D0855096

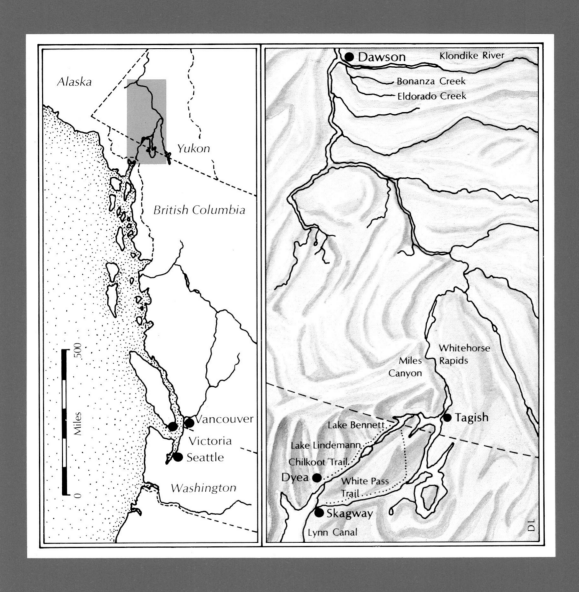

THE KLONDIKE QUEST

A PHOTOGRAPHIC ESSAY

1897~1899

WRITTEN AND EDITED BY

PIERRE BERTON

DESIGN BY FRANK NEWFELD

PHOTOGRAPHIC RESEARCH BY

BARBARA SEARS

MCCLELLAND AND STEWART

COPYRIGHT
© 1983 by Pierre Berton Enterprises Ltd.

Picture Credits

ALL RIGHTS RESERVED

The use of any part of this publication reproduced, transmitted in any form or by any means, electronic, mechanical, photocopying, recording, or otherwise, or stored in a retrieval system, without the prior consent of the publisher is an infringement of the copyright law.

Canadian Cataloguing in Publication Data

Berton, Pierre, 1920-
 The Klondike quest : a photographic essay, 1897-1899

ISBN 0-7710-1288-8

1. Klondike gold rush.* I. Title.

FC4022.3.B37   971.9′102   C83-098070-9
F1095.K5B37

© DESIGN: Frank Newfeld

McClelland and Stewart Limited
The Canadian Publishers

25 Hollinger Road, Toronto,
Ontario M4B 3G2

PRINTED AND BOUND IN HONG KONG
BY EVERBEST PRINTING CO. LTD.

PROVINCIAL ARCHIVES OF ALBERTA,
ERNEST BROWN COLLECTION, EDMONTON:
pp. 13; 14; 15; 238
VANCOUVER CITY ARCHIVES:
pp. 16; 18/19
SEATTLE MUSEUM OF HISTORY
AND INDUSTRY:
pp. 17; 20
UNIVERSITY OF WASHINGTON,
SEATTLE:
pp. 21, top; 22/23; 27; 28/29; 30; 36; 37;
47; 51; 54, centre; 56; 57; 58/59; 65; 66,
bottom; 70/71; 77; 78/79; 80; 81; 82/83;
86/87; 88, bottom left, top centre, top
right; 90/91; 94/95; 100; 100/101; 104;
108/9; 112/13; 127; 128; 152/53; 157;
158/59; 170, centre and right; 171, centre;
179, 182; 190/91; 192/93; 194; 195; 204;
205; 208/9; 218/19; 220; 221; 224; 225;
233
McGILL UNIVERSITY, MONTREAL:
pp. 21, bottom; 150; 151
YUKON ARCHIVES, WHITEHORSE:
pp. 31; 66, top; 69; 76; 89, bottom left;
106; 107; 121; 135; 170, left; 171, left;
176/77
WASHINGTON STATE HISTORICAL
SOCIETY, TACOMA:
pp. 32/33; 38/39; 44/45; 46; 48/49; 52/53;
54, top and bottom; 105; 120; 140/41
PROVINCIAL ARCHIVES OF
BRITISH COLUMBIA, VICTORIA:
pp. 34/35; 50; 73; 89, top left and top
right; 132/33
VANCOUVER PUBLIC LIBRARY:
pp. 55; 74/75; 130/31; 136; 142, bottom;
143; 144, bottom left; 183
LIBRARY OF CONGRESS,
WASHINGTON, D.C.:
pp. 67; 68; 88, bottom left and centre right
McCORD MUSEUM, NOTMAN ARCHIVES,
MONTREAL:
pp. 72; 134; 137; 138; 139; 178; 230/31

NATIONAL FILM BOARD/COLIN LOW,
MONTREAL:
pp. 84/85; 102/3; 114/15; 116/17; 118/19;
129; 160/61; 162/63; 164/65; 166/67; 168;
169; 172/73; 184; 185; 197; 228; 229; 239
PUBLIC ARCHIVES OF CANADA,
OTTAWA:
pp. 88, top left and bottom centre; 93;
110/11; 144, centre left; 145, bottom; 171,
right; 174/75; 180/81; 201; 202; 211;
212/13; 226/27; 232; 240
GLENBOW ARCHIVES, CALGARY:
pp. 92; 146/47
ALASKA HISTORICAL LIBRARY, JUNEAU:
pp. 130; 200
NATIONAL MUSEUMS OF CANADA,
OTTAWA:
pp. 142, top; 144, top left, top right,
bottom right; 145, top left and top
right; 203
AUTHOR'S COLLECTION:
pp. 148/49; 198/99
ROYAL CANADIAN MOUNTED POLICE,
OTTAWA:
pp. 196; 222/23
UNIVERSITY OF TORONTO,
THOMAS FISHER RARE BOOK LIBRARY:
pp. 206/7; 210
DAWSON CITY MUSEUM:
pp. 214/15; 216/17
UNIVERSITY OF ALASKA ARCHIVES,
JUNEAU:
pp. 234/35

With special thanks for their assistance to Dennis Andersen at the Suzzallo Library, University of Washington, and to Rod Slemmons at Argentum Photographic Services, Seattle, for his work on the University of Washington negatives.

Contents

Gold Fever

Something was in the wind that July morning in 1897; the loungers waiting on the San Francisco wharf felt it. But what was it? Was there substance to those tantalizing whispers drifting out of the North? Was there treasure aboard the stubby little steamer, stained and rusty, puffing slowly toward the dockside? The *Excelsior* was nine days out of a distant port on the Bering Sea called St. Michael, near the mouth of a river known as the Yukon. Somewhere along that obscure waterway, so the rumours hinted, something electrifying had happened.

As the ship drew closer, a murmur rose from the crowd. A long line of men in miners' hats was clustered at the deck railing; and now, as individual features began to emerge from the blur, it was seen that these were men aged beyond their years, gaunt and unshaven, their faces leathered by the sun but with eyes that glittered feverishly – picture-book prospectors, in fact. The buzz increased as it was noticed that their tattered clothing was still stained with the mud and clay of some far-off northern valley.

An outlandish scene followed. Down the gangplank they staggered, wrestling with luggage that seemed extraordinarily heavy – old leather grips bursting at the hinges, packing cases about to break apart, bulging valises, blanket rolls barely secured by straps and so heavy that it required two men to hoist each one to the dock.

It dawned on the spellbound onlookers that this was not common baggage: that these suitcases, canvas sacks, old cartons and boxes were stuffed not with socks and shirts but with gold. And these men, who had been paupers a few months before – some driven nearly to suicide by despair – were now rich beyond their wildest fantasies.

In that moment of comprehension, the Klondike stampede began, not quietly or gradually, but instantaneously and with explosive force.

Before the *Excelsior* could turn north again, her agents had been forced to refuse tickets to ten times her passenger list. For *gold* was a magic word in that dark and dreadful decade, which history has mislabelled the Gay Nineties. In those drab years, when depression destroyed hope and men and women literally died in the gutters of starvation, gold was the rarest of prizes, to be hoarded in socks and sugar bowls by those who had lost faith in paper. Now, it appeared, there was a favoured land somewhere beyond the subarctic mists where the treasure lay thickly on the ground waiting to be shovelled into club bags. And anybody could dig it out – a one-time YMCA worker, an ex-laundryman, a former muralist! For such were among the fortunate ones traipsing off to Selby's Smelting Works with their golden burden, a chattering mob at their heels.

By the time a second treasure ship docked at Seattle, two days later, a kind of mass lunacy had seized the continent. Five thousand people jammed Schwabacher's Dock to greet the *Portland* at 6 a.m., July 19; by 9:30, every road leading to the wharfside was crammed with men and animals, carts and drays. It was as if everyone had been waiting for an excuse to break free. Somewhere just beyond the horizon's rim – few knew exactly where – lay wealth, adventure, and, perhaps more important, release from the dreariness of the decade. In the first twenty-four hours, two thousand New Yorkers tried to buy tickets to the Klondike. In the first week, hundreds quit their jobs; within a month tens of thousands had followed suit. Streetcar operators deserted their trams, policemen their beats, pastors their charges. Clerks walked out of offices, salesmen jumped counters, reporters quit their desks. The mayor of Seattle, attending a convention in San Francisco, did not bother to return home but wired in his resignation and joined the herd.

The world caught the disease. Maoris, Kanakas, Scots, and Serbs were infected. People wore buttons proudly proclaiming, "Yes, I'm going this spring"; it was the thing to do. Men in Klondike outfits were treated free in the saloons. Any druggist's clerk, brought up on Ned Buntline dime novels, could walk into a photographer's studio, don the obligatory furs or mackinaw and high boots, and feel that he too was a seasoned prospector heading for high adventure in a magic land.

One million people, it is said, laid plans to go to the Klondike. One hundred thousand actually set off. And so the Klondike saga is a chronicle of humanity in the mass – of thousands squeezed onto wharfs, jamming street corners, choking roadways; of men, women, horses, and dogs crushed together below decks on overloaded steamers; of beaches crowded with prospectors and pack animals; of dense lines of gold seekers struggling up mountain slopes; of rivers and lakes alive with water craft; of gutted valleys buzzing like hives and ramshackle villages bursting into cities. For the next eighteen months, the Yukon interior plateau became a human anthill.

San Francisco, Seattle, Portland, and Victoria teemed with men, every hotel filled to suffocation, the restaurants overtaxed, the lodging-houses roaring. Near the dock areas, a river of humanity moved sluggishly between ten-foot stacks of supplies. Hundreds clogged the roadways dressed in the approved garb (garish mackinaws, wide-brimmed hats, iron-cleated top-boots), buying beasts of burden: dogs, goats, sheep, oxen, burros, mules, ponies, even reindeer and elk – anything on four legs – at outrageous prices. And as they waited for the ships to take them north, as the steerers from the outfitting houses moved among them and the smooth-talking three-card monte men took their savings, they babbled incessantly about gold, caressing the word with tactile adjectives as if the metal were an end in itself and not a means to a better life. The press caught the sensuous sound and reproduced it with such phrases as "rich, yellow gold," "hard, solid gold," "shining gold." It was up there, somewhere, glittering among the mosses.

Blinded by the prospect of gold, the tenderfeet had only the vaguest idea of what lay ahead. Yet almost every man who fought for passage on the leaky boats bound for Skagway and Dyea was convinced that he would return with a fortune. Some even took gunny sacks to hold the nuggets they expected to scoop from the gravels of Bonanza and El-dorado creeks.

In the Yukon, autumn was already in the air, the birches on the hillsides yellowing, the buckbrush on the treeless peaks turning purple, the shallow ponds bearing a thin skin of morning ice. The stampeders had themselves photographed proudly swathed in furs and so must have had some inkling of the conditions facing them: of the numbing cold on the beaches, the winds howling through the passes, the ghostly fog of the northern winter. But fantasy possessed them: it was as if the gold by its very nature – by its glitter, by its shine – could warm them. Experienced voices sounding notes of caution were drowned out by the thunder of the stampede.

The Nineties was the decade of the swindler and the confidence man, and it might be said that every white- and blue-collar worker who joined in the scramble that winter was conning himself. He had to believe he would find what he was seeking, otherwise in conscience he could not go – could not desert his job, his family, his home, for a will-o'-the-wisp beyond the frozen mountains. But *not* to go was unthinkable. So, in that era of insecurity, when mortgages were foreclosed on a whim, when robber barons prospered and most others grew more wretched, when the workhouse, the sweatshop, and the pauper's grave were realities and not figures of speech, each man who set off on the golden trail was forced to believe not only in the future but also in himself. Thus, in an odd way, the Klondike quest wiped out the crisis of confidence that had stultified a continent. "Hurrah for the Klondike!" the crowds on the dock carolled, as each overladen ship limped out of harbour. It was a kind of war cry, a mass paean of hope that somehow, in some magical way, things were going to be better.

Success at the rainbow's end became an article of faith. No scheme was too harebrained, no project too lunatic to shatter the confidence of the true believers. A diver who announced that he would trudge beneath the foaming waters picking up nuggets was taken seriously. So was a man who proposed to suck gold from the creeks using compressed air, and another who claimed to have trained gophers to dig for treasure, and a group of clairvoyants who planned to find the elusive pay-streak by gazing into crystal balls. Scores set off for the promised land on bicycles or on ingenious adaptations of them – on "ice bicycles" or "bicycle skates" – for this was the high point of the velocipede craze. Others planned to soar across the mountains by balloon or chug up the icy passes on motor sledges or snow trains with gigantic sprocket wheels. No device was too bizarre to attract the gullible.

The idea of gold begot gold. Once it had been so scarce that a gold dollar was worth twice as much as a paper dollar, but now the coins came out from beneath the floor boards as the gold seekers spent their hoards on anything bearing the magical name "Klondike" – on Klondike glasses, Klondike medicine chests, even Klondike soup; on anything designed to lighten the burden on the long trail north: coffee lozenges, evaporated eggs, desiccated onions, beef blocks, peanut meal, saccharine and pemmican; and on less practical devices: mechanical gold pans, nugget-in-the-slot machines, patented gold rockers, collapsible beds, knockdown boats, portable cabins, scurvy cures, even x-ray machines designed to detect the presence of the golden treasure hidden in the dross.

Like those thrill seekers who gaped at the astonishing illusions of the stage magicians, the stampeders were caught up in the willing suspension of disbelief. There were those who set off for the mystic land of gold as blithely as they might depart for London, Paris, or Bombay. They took caged canaries, parrots, upright pianos, portable bowling alleys, lawn tennis sets, magic lanterns. The marvel is that some of this bric-à-brac actually reached the city of gold. Some of it is there to this day.

Their optimism was unparalleled, and that is strange because theirs was not an optimistic age. But it was an age of yearning, and the Klondike had taken on a mythic aura. It was more than a goldfield, more than a piece of geography: it was Beulahland, the panacea to all the fears and torments of the era, an answer for the lonely, an inspiration to the God-fearing, a bulwark against the frailties of the flesh. For if the creek beds were said to be paved with gold, were not also the streets of the New Jerusalem?

Thus, no one was much surprised when the Beecher Memorial Church of Brooklyn announced that it would build a second Brooklyn in the clear air of the Yukon, free of drinkers, gamblers, and non-Christians, at the foot of "a mountain which is said to be the fountainhead of the goldfield"; or when a leading sociologist developed a scheme to transport four thousand spinsters from the sweatshops of New England to the free and open spaces of the Klondike; or when a Pittsburgh promoter launched a matrimonial agency to secure jobs in the promised land for one hundred "poor but respectable women"; or when the Bowery Mission of New York dispatched an expedition north headed by a reformed gambler, charged with converting his fellow stampeders as well as digging for gold.

So strong was their faith in the magic of the Klondike that five hundred widows seeking rich husbands chartered a steamer and set off from New York round the Horn for the goldfields, and in spite of shipwreck and Patagonian cannibals managed to limp into Seattle before their funds were dissipated and their dreams shattered.

Few knew exactly where the Klondike was, and, perhaps because they feared the truth, a surprising number did not bother to find out. A man who planned a regular balloon route to the Klondike–the round trip, he said, would occupy a fortnight–was besieged with offers from hundreds who had obviously never consulted a map. And there were other schemes, equally nutty: a reindeer service modelled on the pony express; a bicycle path to the goldfields to service a chain of trading posts; even a postal system using carrier pigeons.

This blindness to geography was a symptom of the fever that gripped the continent. One Canadian syndicate actually received a government charter to build a railway across seven hundred miles of unmapped tundra from Hudson Bay to Great Slave Lake and on to Dawson, a journey that an enthusiastic Toronto newspaper reported would take a mere seven days. There was something about the Klondike disease that caused normally rational businessmen to abandon all reason and indulge in pipedreams. But then these fantasies were abetted by those who saw profit in madness and gold in gold fever: outfitters, eager to turn a dollar; Chamber of Commerce boosters, booming their communities; promoters organizing syndicates for cash on the barrelhead. For every man in the crowd scrambling northward seeking a gold mine, there was at least one shill on the lookout for a mark.

In the coastal cities the crowds on the docks were so desperate for berths on any vessel going north that scores refused to give up their places in the queue to eat or sleep. Thousands fought for tickets or robbed those who had tickets or bribed their way aboard the floating coffins struggling along the ravelled coast of British Columbia and past the fiords and glaciers of the Alaska panhandle. On these patched-up craft, once condemned to the boneyard, now resurrected to fill the demand, conditions were such that by comparison penal servitude must have seemed almost jolly. Some passengers were packed in ten to a cabin, on bunks of rough lumber; others lived in suffocating holds or on the deck even in the driving rain. They slept in their clothes, waited seven hours for an execrable meal, suffered storms, explosions, starvation, shipwreck, mutiny, and mayhem. Dogs died in their crates, men were swept overboard in storms, horses kicked each other into insensibility, and yet the stampeders suffered it all – suffered the stench of manure and vomit, the continual yapping and howling of pack dogs, the dreadful claustrophobia below decks, the choking clouds of coal dust, the groaning and creaking of the leaky hulls, and, above all, the sweat of their fellow men, packed tightly like so many herring for days, even weeks, on end. They suffered it because, at the end of the ghastly sea journey, the beaches of Skagway and Dyea beckoned. And beyond the beaches lay the mountain trails. And beyond the trails lay the passes. And beyond the passes lay the frozen lakes. And beyond the lakes lay the great river. And at the river's end lay Mecca.

Posing against painted backgrounds in the studios of coastal photographers, thousands of aspiring adventurers, eager to get rich, demonstrated their optimism by commissioning portraits of themselves on the eve of their departure for the goldfields – mementoes for friends and families and visual proof that they had no intention of being left behind in the race.

Fake snow scenes, potted palms, bogus fences and fireplaces – the props of the Victorian photo studio – were no stranger than those costumes affected by some who had no conception of northern conditions or the Yukon's winter climate. It's doubtful that the dogs seen here ever made it to the Klondike – or the violin, either, for that matter.

The return of prosperity

The Klondike boom rescued the West Coast cities from depression. On Vancouver's Cordova Street *(opposite)*, outfitters did a roaring trade in fur coats, mackinaws, sledges, boots, and more exciting items such as clockwork gold pans operating on a spindle on the gramophone principle. The docks in all the coastal cities, and the streets leading to them, were so crowded that traffic could scarcely move as men and women fought for passage on ancient ships once condemned to the scrapyard.

Rudolph Nyman   J.H.

Yukon Adventure 1

OUTFITTING CO

Mr Coffee & Green

'98 Vancouver BC

A grotesque flotilla

Any patched-up vessel that could be resurrected was pressed into service on the Pacific Coast run. Yachts, sloops, barques, scows, barges, steamboats, sailing schooners all headed north crammed with men and animals. The *Bristol (lower right)* was one of the first out of Victoria, with six hundred horses jammed into two-foot stalls on deck – so badly overloaded that she almost turned turtle a few miles out of port and was forced to creep back to harbour to readjust her topload. The passengers were squeezed into rough bunks that filled every corner of the ship. Even that didn't meet the demand. The ship attempted to tow a stern-wheel steamboat behind her with such lamentable results that the craft had to be cut adrift off Vancouver Island.

2 The Shimmering Sands

The beaches of Skagway and Dyea lay at the end of one of the world's most beautiful fiords, the ninety-mile-long Lynn Canal. Here the mountain slopes, rising sheer from the turquoise waters, were perfectly reflected in the polished sea. Dusted with new snow, they dwarfed the tiny, imperfect vessels steaming up the alpine corridor.

The men on board those vessels had little appetite for natural grandeur, for to them the scenery was an obstacle. For some, it was the first jolt of reality after weeks of fantasizing. At last they realized that the journey to the land of gold would be no easy stroll. Barring the way was a massive bulwark of ice and granite, from whose toothed crest cataracts roared and tumbled and vast glaciers hung suspended. The spectacle of this chill barrier banished forever the pipedreams that had titillated the optimists. No bicycle or boatsled could breach it; no balloon could soar over it; no carrier pigeon would dare cross it. Staring up at those forbidding ramparts the stampeders realized that they would have to make the attempt themselves, on foot or perhaps on horseback, through one of the two narrow gaps in the mountains—the White and the Chilkoot passes.

But to reach the passes, each man must disembark with his outfit and his animals and make his way through one of two new boom towns: Dyea, at the start of the Chilkoot trail, or Skagway, three miles to the west at the foot of the White Pass. Here was a second shock. Crowding along the deck rail, the first newcomers could hear the anchor drop and the engines shudder to a stop; but the land was more than a mile away, and there was no sign of a wharf—only a huddle of shacks among the trees in the far distance. No gangplank here; no porters to help with the luggage; no waiting charabancs; no stevedores, either (they had long since deserted for the goldfields); only the interminable tidal flats and the sodden beaches, veined by glacial rivulets.

Over the side they went, men, horses, dogs, and baggage, into the freezing ocean or into the snub-nosed scows shuttling back and forth to the beaches. Horses, snorting in terror, were suspended over the side in boxes whose bottoms swung open, plunging the struggling animals into waters already alive with goats, mules, dogs, and oxen. Trunks were hurled into waiting scows with such force that they often burst apart. Packing cases splintered as they landed. Entire outfits were thrown unceremoniously onto the sands in total disorder until each beach became a chaos of boxes, flour sacks, frying pans, sheet-iron stoves, upturned boats, wagons, piles of hay, and heaps of luggage. Like rats in a labyrinth, men scurried about seeking their belongings, some clambering to the tops of the mountains of supplies, barking out the names on each container, and throwing down the goods to the crowd below.

Nor was this the worst of their problems. The tide was inexorable; it could rise as much as thirty feet with tragic results. And so, as each vessel disgorged its cargo, the beaches were never still. Dogs yelped, wagons creaked, saws rasped, campfires sputtered, horses neighed, and men cursed as they struggled to move their goods above the high-water mark before the creeping waters reduced them all to mush. Some, beaten by the advancing sea, flung themselves onto the sand and sobbed as the salt water engulfed the flour, sugar, oatmeal, baking soda, salt, yeast, dried potatoes, and desiccated soup on which they had squandered their savings.

Beyond the beaches, the twin communities began to swell yeastily out of the shattered forest, each crammed with men frantic to move on up the trails, over the passes, and down the river to Dawson before freeze-up. There was no law. As the pressure from the human flood increased, the buildings of the early pioneers were moved unceremoniously or dynamited to suit the convenience of the newcomers. Lined by makeshift saloons, the main streets were ruts of black mud down which rivers of men and animals ceaselessly flowed. And with each passing day, the stampeders who had looted their sugar bowls to finance the treasure hunt found their resources dwindling.

There were those who quickly saw where the real treasure lay – not beneath the frozen mosses of Eldorado Creek, half a thousand miles away, but here in the pockets of those who still believed in Eldorado. Behind the ramshackle fronts of the two towns, mingling with the scraping of fiddles, the hammering of pianos, and the laughter of easy women, subtler sounds could be heard: the whir of the wheel, the click of the chips. Three-card monte men abounded; phoney information offices did a land-office business; fake telegraph clerks sent fake telegraphs at a one-hundred-per-cent profit, for there was no wire linking Alaska with the outside world.

Those who resisted the seductions of the flesh still found their pocketbooks growing thinner. They had been lured north with visions of gold littering the streets, but now at every turn they were hounded for money – for lighterage, for camping space, for fodder, for customs duty, for a bath, for a haircut, for laundry. In San Francisco that year, a square meal cost a quarter; on the Dyea trail, a plate of bacon and beans went for ten times that. In Seattle, a quart of whiskey cost forty cents; in Skagway, you paid more than that for a two-ounce shot. In Victoria, an all-wool suit sold for four dollars, vest and all; in Toronto, a four-room apartment could be had for a dollar a week; but in Skagway, hay cost one hundred and fifty dollars a ton, and in Dyea, a man would have to give close to a month's wages to have his horse shod.

"Take your photograph, sir?"

"Of course!"

"Cash on the line, please!"

Pay to pose once again against a fake background or an outdoor shack, smiling optimistically or looking suitably grim and dashing in your new outfit. Something to send back home to keep up the spirits of those left behind. And why not? There *is* gold at the end of the trail; everybody says so.

But not for those with "icicle feet" – men so called because they had reached the end of their tether. Their only remaining asset was the half-ton of goods they had brought with them, and so they opened temporary restaurants in tattered tents or frame shelters to peddle the bacon, beans, and tea that they had purchased at such cost. With that meagre profit they bought a return ticket home and picked their way for the last time across the littered beaches to the water line to heave themselves aboard a waiting scow.

Even as they did so scores of others disembarked and, with eyes shining and hearts thumping, pushed on to join the endless chain of men and women greedily trudging northward through the wet sand and the yellow gumbo and the rapidly falling snow, up through the forest and into the canyons, along the trail of dead horses.

LYNN CANAL AND SKAGWAY FROM MT. DEWEY.

The end of one journey,
the start of another

The boom town of Skagway occupied a tidal flat at the top of the lovely Alaskan fiord known as the Lynn Canal. On the extreme right, a second arm of the fiord reached the mouth of the Dyea River where the twin boom town of that name sprang up. The Klondikers could choose to land at Skagway *(left)* and head up toward the White Pass, or take the Dyea trail to the Chilkoot.

80.A.
W&S

DYEA BEACH   ALASKA

The sands of Dyea

When they first saw this desert of sand
and mud at the mouth of the Dyea
River, the newcomers were shocked.
The ships anchored far out in the bay,
and each man had to trundle his goods
across this wet expanse to a point
above the high-water mark, otherwise
the sea would roll over his cartons
of dried foods. Some men used horses or
dogs to help them, but many had only their
own backs. There was more than one
who lost the battle with the advancing
tide, lost not only the possessions he
had saved and scrimped for – desiccated
soup, flour, yeast, salt, tea – but also his
chance to push on toward the goldfields.
For the Yukon interior was empty of food.
No man could enter without a year's
supply. Here, for many, the dream ended.

At Dyea, flat-bottomed scows were used
to shuttle the stampeders' goods from ship
to shore – but always for a hefty fee.

At Skagway, the scene was almost identical. Some men hired boats and poled their goods to shore. Others used teams of horses that waded in the shallow waters, heading for a ragged line of tents.

46104
ASAHEL CURTIS

Mushrooming Skagway

Like every booming community along the Klondike trails, Skagway began as a tent town. The picture on the left was taken in August, 1897, the one on the right two months later. The leading saloon was operated by Frank and John Clancy, key figures in the community's palmy days and supporters of Jefferson Randolph "Soapy" Smith, the confidence man who became Skagway's dictator. A year later, Smith met his death in a gunfight.

At the start of the trail

Only after leaving the beaches did the Klondikers begin to comprehend the travail that faced them. Ahead lay a narrow footpath, viscous with slime and shale, snaking upward toward the summit. Each must climb the mountain, flogging his horses or driving his dogs – slipping, sliding, sometimes tumbling – not once but many times as he shuttled his ton of goods forward, a few pounds at a time, through rain, sleet, and blizzard, as part of an impersonal chain of groaning animals and humans.

3　The Trail of Dead Horses

The trail that led out of Skagway toward the White Pass was deceptive. It looked so easy at the outset – a pleasant wagon road winding between the tall pines, an easy jaunt on horseback on the route to the rainbow's end. Then came Devil's Hill, and the horror began. The road was no longer a road, only a narrow path, scarcely two feet wide, that twisted and corkscrewed for forty-five miles through an appalling series of mountain barriers, each more dismaying than the last. Here were precipices of slippery slate where a misstep could mean a five-hundred-foot plunge to death. Here were rivulets of liquid mud, coursing down the mountainside. Here were sinkholes that could swallow a horse, pack and all; and razor-sharp rocks that tore at the feet; and vast fields of boulders, ten feet high, through which the pack animals groped and stumbled.

By mire and bog, by canyon and riverbed, by slope and summit, the fantastic serpent moved in agonizing fits and starts through a sunless drizzle – a hopeless tangle of men and animals, ankle deep in slime, the humans cursing and groaning as they tried to urge their pack animals forward.

Clinging to the boulder-strewn slopes of Porcupine Hill, those who dared to look below were treated to a grisly sight. Three thousand horses were to die on the White Pass trail that winter. Their rotting cadavers could already be seen strewn along the gravels of the Skagway River, a pitiful hedgerow of carrion leading upward toward the summit of the pass.

Some animals, badly loaded, died violently, losing their balance and plunging from the cliff edge to the waters below. Some died of fever brought on by lacerated hoofs, tattered on the sharp rocks of the trail, or by running sores suffered at the hands of amateurs who did not know how to load a pack. Some vanished in mudholes or were drowned in the river.

Others died of poison or starvation or were beaten to death by men trying vainly to urge them onward. Many died of exhaustion, standing fully loaded for as long as twenty hours at a stretch while their masters waited for the human chain to resume its slow progress. One or two, it was said, actually committed suicide by flinging themselves over a cliff. A few were shot out of compassion; but that was rare, for the men struggling up toward the White Pass seemed to have been squeezed dry of their ration of human sentiment. In Jack London's words, and he was a witness there that fall, "Their hearts turned to stone–those which did not break–and they became beasts, the men on the Dead Horse Trail."

Perhaps it was the misty half-light that distorted human sensibility. Men and animals moved as if drugged through a funereal drizzle. In this unreal world, where campfires sputtered wanly like ghost lights in the mist, exhausted men, thwarted by the snail-like progress of the living escalator, were driven to the pit of brutality. Unwilling to blame themselves, they blamed their animals and in a kind of delirium worked out their frustrations on the nearest pack horse. Like exasperated motorists who honk their horns in a traffic snarl, they beat their animals unmercifully and when the beasts could go no farther left them to expire on the trail, where the human machine, unheeding and uncaring, trampled them into porridge.

It was asking too much of nature. By September the trail had become impassable, and the line ground to a stop. It had become obvious that no one else could get through to the Klondike before spring. As the trail closed, the weeding-out process began again. Thousands retreated to Skagway and tried to sell that portion of their outfits that had not been left behind. For forty miles the trail was strewn with the discarded goods of those who could go no farther and whose pack horses had given up the ghost.

In the lull that followed, a thousand surviving animals blackened Skagway's tidal flats, their backs lacerated, the blood pouring down their flanks, "For Sale" signs hanging over their manes. Newcomers bought them cheaply and tried to keep them alive until the gumbo froze and the river turned to ice and the great serpent could resume its slow passage through a thickening curtain of falling snow.

Now it was made clear to the stampeders that they could not cross the summit into Canadian territory without a year's supply of provisions. In the interior of the Yukon, every scrap of food had been devoured by the early birds; any man who didn't pack in a ton of supplies–more than half of it food–would freeze and starve in an empty domain devoid of outfitters, grocery stores, provisioners, and transport. And so the men from the big cities who had thought of the trek to the Klondike in terms of a headlong dash – paddling like fury across lakes and down rivers in a race for treasure – now found themselves trapped in a maddeningly slow shuttle. Few could carry more than sixty-five pounds at a time, and so they moved in five-mile stages, caching each parcel of goods and returning for another load, over and over again. Some men covered twenty-five hundred miles on foot before reaching Lake Bennett. Even those fortunate enough to drag weightier loads on sledges took a minimum of ninety days to go through the White Pass.

With thousands of feet hammering the snow into white granite and with more snow falling daily, the trail assumed a shape of its own, rising inch by inch, hard as concrete, until in places it was ten feet higher than the surrounding terrain. Along the crest of this great white pipeline men slipped and slithered, as in a chain gang, packed so tightly that the queue could pass a given point for five hours straight without a break appearing. There was no level spot to stop and rest, and those unlucky ones who slipped off the trail might wait for half a day before finding a gap in the line into which they could squeeze. Bent almost double, breath frozen, face purple with strain, each man became an anonymous link in the chain, submerging his personality into the all-encompassing coil that wound upward to the summit. Gasping as they dragged their sledges, groaning under the weight of their packs, cursing their dogs and pack animals, they staggered forward, their muffled voices rising in concert through the thin air to mingle into an all-encompassing moan, which, like some spectral organ note, penetrated the mists below and rose in a low wail to the topmost peaks of the White Pass.

For every man who reached the summit, another turned back. Some threw themselves, exhausted, onto the side of the trail and gave up. Some grew deathly ill from the rotten horsemeat served in trailside cafés. Some sickened and died from grippe, pneumonia, or meningitis. Some ran out of food and could go no farther. Some were turned back by the North West Mounted Police, who guarded the border.

Others refused to admit defeat. One used a string of reindeer to haul his supplies through the pass. Another, a woman, strapped dough to her back, which – after it rose with the heat of her body and was made into bread – she sold at a handsome profit. One man and his wife actually moved two stern-wheel steamboats in pieces over the summit. A photographer, E.A. Hegg, with a sleigh pulled by a team of long-haired goats, supported himself taking photographs; displayed later in a Broadway emporium, these pictures of dead animals and gaunt, vacant-eyed men caused a sensation. The Klondike creeks were still half a year away, but these entrepreneurs had already found their Bonanza.

And then there were those who simply could not be discouraged, who saw the Klondike experience as an enormous adventure to be relished and enjoyed for its own sake, who met adversity on its own terms and surmounted it – like the group of Scots, in furs and tam-o'-shanters, who crossed the pass that winter led by a piper, skirling away among the mountain peaks and down the long slope that led at last to the shores of Lake Bennett. Here the boat builders were already at work, preparing for the spring breakup and the next leg of the weary trek to the goldfields.

Toward the White Pass

The trail to the summit of the
White Pass was no trail at all,
only a jumble of shattered rock
and broken deadfalls over which
men and pack animals were
forced to claw their way.
"This accursed trail," as one
stampeder called it, brought out
the worst in men, driving them
into a kind of delirium that
made them worse than brutes.
"I am undoubtedly a crazy fool
for being here in this God-
forsaken country," one wrote home,
"but I have the consolation of
seeing thousands of other men
in all stages of life, rich and
poor, wise and foolish, here
in the same plight as I."

46110
ASAHEL CURTIS

Every horse that travelled the White Pass trail was doomed. "Such a scene of havoc and destruction...can scarcely be imagined," wrote one man. "Thousands of packhorses lie dead along the way, sometimes in bunches under the cliffs....The inhumanity...the heartbreak...cannot be imagined."

At Little Lake on the White Pass trail, a pack train comes to a dead stop. None of these animals will survive.

On Porcupine Hill, where horses must pick their way between ten-foot boulders, the queue again stops dead.

The weary climb to the summit

When the snow fell and the mud froze, the White Pass trail, which had been closed for months, reopened. Even with the help of oxen, horses, and sledges, men under the strain of returning again and again for a new load – only to find it buried under a dozen feet of snow – were driven to lunacy. One, having reached the summit at last, gave his dogs a savage beating; then, when they could go no farther, he drowned them one by one through a waterhole in the ice before collapsing in tears. Another built a fire under an ox that would not move and roasted the beast alive. Yet few paid any attention to these horrors. A dead man with a hole in his back lay beside the trail for hours. The stampeders paid him no heed but pushed on by fits and starts – dark, satanic figures limned against the alabaster of the mountain slopes.

LOOKING DOWN THROUGH CUTOFF CANYON FROM HALF MILE BELOW WHITE PASS SUMMIT.

Guarding the border

At the summit of the pass a detachment of North West Mounted Police stood guard with a Maxim gun on orders from the Canadian government. The boundary was in dispute, the Americans trying to push it back to the headwaters of the Yukon, the Canadians insisting it lay close to the seashore. Finally the police established a customs house on the crest of the divide. Here firewood and building logs had to be fetched from twelve miles below. Here the snow fell almost ceaselessly. And here the climbers found they had to pay duty on every pound of supplies dragged at such cost to the summit. Possession being nine points of the law, the international border was eventually established here, where the police had seized it and held it for Canada.

UNION JACK, AND STARS AND STRIPES ON THE WHITE PASS

SNOW STORM ON THE SUMMIT OF WHITE PASS.   COPY

On the White Pass summit, an endless blizzard

Few men lingered long after they reached the top of the pass. The snow fell thickly, night and day, covering packs, equipment, tents, and shacks. The stampeders headed back down the slopes for another load or pushed on toward Lake Bennett, where the weather was milder. But for the detachment of twenty Mounted Policemen there was no release. The health of many was permanently damaged. Working waist deep in snow and melt water, encased in frozen clothes, they were racked by influenza and bronchitis. Yet they stayed at their post, standing on guard for their country, giving aid and advice to the thousands of men and women – mostly foreigners – who stumbled about in the white fog of winter like lost souls trapped in a Dantesque purgatory.

59

4 Up the Golden Stairs

The questing throngs who found themselves dumped onto the beaches at the head of the Lynn Canal had two choices. They could opt for the Skagway trail with its rivers of mud and its stench of carrion, or they could join the human torrent pouring through Dyea and set out along the winding Dyea River to assault the dizzier heights of the Chilkoot.

Appearances were always deceptive on the trails of Ninety-eight. The Chilkoot Pass was six hundred feet higher than the White. No loaded pack animal could negotiate that last precipitous ascent–a jumble of slippery, house-sized boulders in autumn, a terrifying incline of sheer ice in winter. Yet in spite of thundering avalanches and shrieking gales, the Chilkoot proved to be the most effective gateway to the goldfields. Of those who attacked it, some twenty-two thousand eventually made it to the other side, each with his ton of supplies.

Out of Dyea they streamed, into the meadows and forests of the river delta. After the anarchy of the boom town the peace of the Dyea Valley brought temporary quiet. The wagon road meandered deceptively back and forth across the riverbed, through rustling copses of cottonwood, spruce, birch, and willow.

But each man as he trudged forward, hauling his goods by wagon or handcart, began to encounter the familiar litter of the stampede and to realize that the Dyea trail was not what it seemed. Strewn by the wayside were scores of trunks, the most impractical of all baggage, some still filled with cheap jewellery, souvenirs, trinkets, and framed photographs that no longer had any value for those whose minds were obsessed with richer booty. As the grade grew sharper the river was squeezed into a gloomy canyon; emerging, each man began to feel the tug of gravity. Directly ahead the chiselled mountains of the Coastal series barred the way. At their base, at the margin of the timber line – the last place on the trail where firewood or lumber could be obtained – stood Sheep Camp.

Here, in a deep basin scooped from the encircling mountains, each new arrival was exposed to a humbling spectacle, one he would never forget: before him, the huddle of frame hovels and soiled tents; beyond and above, hanging from a notch in the peaks, a continuous ribbon of climbers draped across the whitewashed slopes. In that sunless world the scene was two dimensional, for the shadowless incline seemed devoid of relief save for that dark garland being drawn upward, as if in slow motion, toward the summit.

Now each man realized the dimensions of the effort required of him. The summit was only a four-mile crow's flight away, but it was thirty-five hundred feet above the town of Dyea. Soon, he too would be a flyspeck on that wall of ice.

Sheep Camp was never still – shifting, expanding, and contracting with the human tide, a bedlam of sweating men, howling dogs, and abandoned horses. And here, as elsewhere, the barest necessities became luxuries. Here were fifteen hotels, none worthy of the name, where an exhausted man could pay two days' wages for a single meal or a small fortune for the privilege of sleeping on the floor, jammed so tightly against his fellows that by nightfall no one could stand up, enter, or leave. And here you could buy anything from candy and nuts to kitchenware and firewood, as long as you were able to pay. You could buy a woman for five dollars, and many men, staring upward at that thirty-five-degree slope and hungry for one final fling, did just that.

Each man setting out from Sheep Camp could see that there were two places only on the four-mile climb where he could properly rest. The first lay beneath a gigantic boulder known as the Stone House. The second was a flat ledge called the Scales, at the very base of the steepest ascent. Here the professional packers re-weighed their loads, increasing the tariff to a dollar a pound. An exhausted tenderfoot, shuttling his ton of supplies a load at a time up the Chilkoot, was faced here with a bill for two thousand dollars if he felt he could go no farther: it was either pay, pack, or quit. No animal could carry or haul a load past the Scales, and only a few horses made the climb unloaded. Everything – including sledges and dogs – must be carried over on men's backs. And so, as the snow fell ceaselessly, small mountains of supplies began to grow at the Scales as their owners shuttled back and forth from Sheep Camp and gathered their energies for the final climb.

From the Scales to the summit, from dawn until dusk, the line was never broken as the men, bent double, inched forward in an odd rhythmic motion that came to be called the Chilkoot Lockstep. None would ever forget the experience, and in the years to come one sound would continue to echo in their memories – the single, all-encompassing groan, which, as on the White Pass trail, rose from the bowl of the mountains like the hum of a thousand insects.

Alternately sweating and freezing in the heavy furs and woollens in which they had once been photographed so jauntily, jackknifed by the pull of gravity for eight hours a day, unable to undress or bathe, terrorized by howling winds and the fear of avalanches, half starved on skimpy meals of cold beans, soggy flapjacks, and bad coffee, drained by dysentery and stomach cramps, they struggled up the "Golden Stairs" – fifteen hundred steps cut out of the sheer ice, with a single ice-sheathed rope to cling to.

The interminable delays brought on by blizzards and mishaps on the trail drove them to agonies of frustration. Yet this might have been endured had it not been for the terrible truth that faced each one who finally reached the wind-blown summit and deposited his fifty pounds of supplies (few could carry more) among the pyramids of chattels already half smothered by the falling snow. Exhausted by the climb – filthy, stinking, red-eyed, and bone-weary – each knew that this was but the beginning, that he must go down again and up again, again and again and again, until he had checked it all through the Mounted Police post at the border: bacon and tea, flour and beans, clothing, tents, stove, sledge. There were no hardware stores on the far side where the headwater lakes awaited the onslaught of the gold seekers. All the tools needed to build a boat – whipsaw, whetstone, hatchet, drawknife, chisel, nails, jackplane, and square – all these had to accompany each climber along with coils of rope, buckets of pitch and oakum, and, most important of all, the inevitable gold pan. For without his personal pan how could a man dip into the golden creeks of the Klondike and wash out a fortune?

Until the first crude tramway was opened in December (there were five operating by May, 1898), every pound had to be lugged up the slope and deposited at the summit on men's backs. For those who could not afford to pay the Indian packers this added up to forty trips in all. Given the weather, it meant that the average man took at least three months to get his goods up the Golden Stairs.

At the summit a city of goods took shape, supplies piled up like buildings, with narrow passageways like streets wriggling between them and a forest of long-handled shovels poking up through the snow to mark each property. Soon the blanket of falling snow covered even these markers, burying everything – pianos and liquor kegs, timber and glassware, crates of fine silk and barrels of stuffed turkeys, even a plough weighing 125 pounds, carried up the slope on a wager by a farm boy from Iowa.

Again there were those who saw that the real gold was closer than the Klondike and who were determined to pay their way as they went, calling on the laws of supply and demand to enrich them: a sackful of old newspapers, a grindstone, ten thousand bottles of mosquito lotion – these luxuries, lugged up the Golden Stairs by would-be entrepreneurs, would soon be worth more than their weight in gold. One woman paid her way by giving concerts on a banjo, another by selling whiskey from a portable bar, the price rising with the steepness of the slope. But for those who expected to dig a fortune from the goldfields, cost was immaterial. The climbers paid hard cash to see a man shoot spots off a playing card at fifty feet; they paid tolls to use the steps in the ice; and when they reached the top, they paid a dollar a pound for firewood and two dollars for a stale doughnut and a cup of weak coffee. And to the Mounted Police manning the customs tent, they paid duty on every pound of goods carried at such cost over the Canadian border.

Some paid more and got nothing in return. All along the Chilkoot trail the confidence men waited for the suckers, building fires to warm them, constructing wayside ledges to take the weight of their burdens, raising tents to shield them from the gale. Disguised as fellow climbers, hauling fake sledges – mere hollow cages with pick handles protruding from them – or carrying packs filled with feathers, they seemed to be Good Samaritans playing parlour games. But the pea was never to be discovered beneath the shell, and the men seeking riches were always poorer for the encounter.

Yet no mountebank could dampen their ardour for long. Over and over again they struggled upward, forced almost to their knees by the steepness of the slope, until they seemed like suppliants before an altar. Hardship served only to fuel their fanaticism; personal tragedies along the way only hardened their hearts. One man lay beside the trail for a day in agony from a broken leg; they paid him no heed, trudging on unseeing, until a professional packer carried him back down the mountain.

Mishap, accident, sickness, death, even murder did not move them. But theft drove them to a fury, for theft was the most heinous of crimes that winter. A man who had his outfit stolen knew that he had lost his chance at fortune's wheel; the Mounties would turn him back at the border. Then it was all for nothing: the months of preparation, the applause of friends and family, the coastal hardships, the struggle on the beaches, the weary climb up the Golden Stairs. Any man caught stealing could expect swift justice: to be stripped to the waist, tied to a post, and lashed unmercifully. Rather than face this torture one thief blew his head off. "He that maketh haste to be rich shall not be unpunished," said the clergyman who buried him. Few caught the unwitting irony of that text.

Two dreadful accidents bracketed that manic winter. In September, a prodigious glacier that hung over the pass was loosened by heavy rain. The autumn winds ripped away half an acre of ice, releasing thousands of gallons of melt water. Roaring down the trail, a terrifying wave twenty feet high picked up the Stone House as if it were a pebble and sent it tumbling a quarter of a mile down the valley. Forty outfits and three men were lost.

The following April, more than sixty were smothered to death as thousands of tons of wet snow were suddenly dislodged from a peak twenty-five hundred feet above the trail. As scores fled back toward Sheep Camp, the gargantuan mass descended, burying everything in its path, until an area ten acres in size was covered to a depth of ten feet. Only a few emerged from beneath this suffocating blanket. The others died because they had refused to listen to the warnings of the Indian packers that the pass should be shunned that day. Frustrated by two weeks of bad weather that had kept them off the trail, lured by a lull in the storms, and goaded by the insistent pull of their own aspirations, they dared to attempt the pass until a moving wall of snow obliterated them.

Next day the line of strugglers resumed its slow upward crawl. Above them, at the summit, the snow had reached a depth of seventy feet. Here the pass was a trench one hundred yards wide through which blizzards whistled incessantly, blotting out all vision and creating a spectral world in which the blurred shapes of men moved like apparitions, seeking goods and chattels buried under perhaps seven storeys of snow. Only when the spring sun began to melt that crusting mantle could they pack up once more and head off toward the lakes, twelve hundred feet below, from which the faint sound of hammer and whipsaw told them that a gigantic armada was in the making.

Horses could traverse only the lower part of the Dyea trail. Eventually all the goods had to be carried on the backs of men.

An ungainly cart with wooden wheels carries one party's outfit up the
easy incline of the Dyea Valley. Soon, however, the cart, the rocking chair,
and even the dog will have to be discarded as gravity exerts its pull.

Men and horses wade in the shallow Dyea River at the start of the Chilkoot
trail while others camp comfortably beneath overhanging rocks. But the
horses will be useless farther on – as will that heavy packing-case table.

The first major obstacle on the trail that led to the Chilkoot was the canyon through which the Dyea River roared and tumbled. The stampeders were forced to haul their goods across makeshift bridges over icicle-sheathed fissures and through a clutter of boulders, fallen trees, and tangled roots. Yet this was a Sunday stroll compared to what they were to face.

Bringing
the word of God
to the Klondike

In a frozen hollow in the Coastal Mountains, not far from Sheep Camp, the Reverend Hall Young, one of Alaska's best-known Protestant ministers, sets up camp with his party. Young was in the vanguard of Christian missionaries heading for the goldfields (although Roman Catholics and Anglicans had been on the scene years before the great strike). He made it over the Chilkoot Pass well before winter closed in and opened Dawson's first Presbyterian church in a cabin rented from a saloonkeeper. Young is on the left in this photograph, a tough, sinewy man of God, the embodiment of the "muscular Christian" so beloved by the Victorian age. The guns are for hunting food, not for sport.

The scales of commerce...

At Sheep Camp, every pound of goods is weighed by those who can afford professional packers. Before the last ascent it will all be weighed again.

...and of justice

A thief named Hansen, caught and
sentenced by miners' court, is stripped
and given 15 lashes near Sheep Camp.
The date was February 15, 1898.

Death on the slopes

On April 3, 1898, a terrifying avalanche of snow hurtled down from a peak 2,500 feet overhead. A thirty-foot layer buried scores, but within 20 minutes a thousand men arrived from Sheep Camp with shovels. There were many miraculous rescues, including that of an ox that lived for two days in a natural cave under the snow. At least sixty men perished.

Released from one frozen grave, the stiffened corpses of the slide victims were soon given burial in another. When spring arrived, the new tomb became a lake of melt water, its surface bobbing with bloated cadavers.

The scene
from the Scales

In a mountain hollow a weird
community known as the Scales
took shape – so called because all
supplies must be re-weighed here
before the professional packers
would handle them. Now the
stampeders, struggling up from
Sheep Camp, could see all too
plainly the trials that lay ahead.
The shortest route to the summit
was on the left – an incline of
thirty-five degrees; no pack
animal could negotiate it. On the
right was a longer trail down
which many men came sliding on
their shovels before heading back
up with another fifty pounds.
Here is the great panorama
of the Klondike stampede, the
symbolic spectacle that, in
a single frame, mirrors all the
hope and despair of the great
gold rush: men, like suppliants
before an altar, bent double
under their burdens, striving
ever upward toward a goal that
was more illusory than real.
The Golden Stairs, they called
them. Most men were forced to
climb them forty times – those
who did not give up and return
to the warmth of their homes.

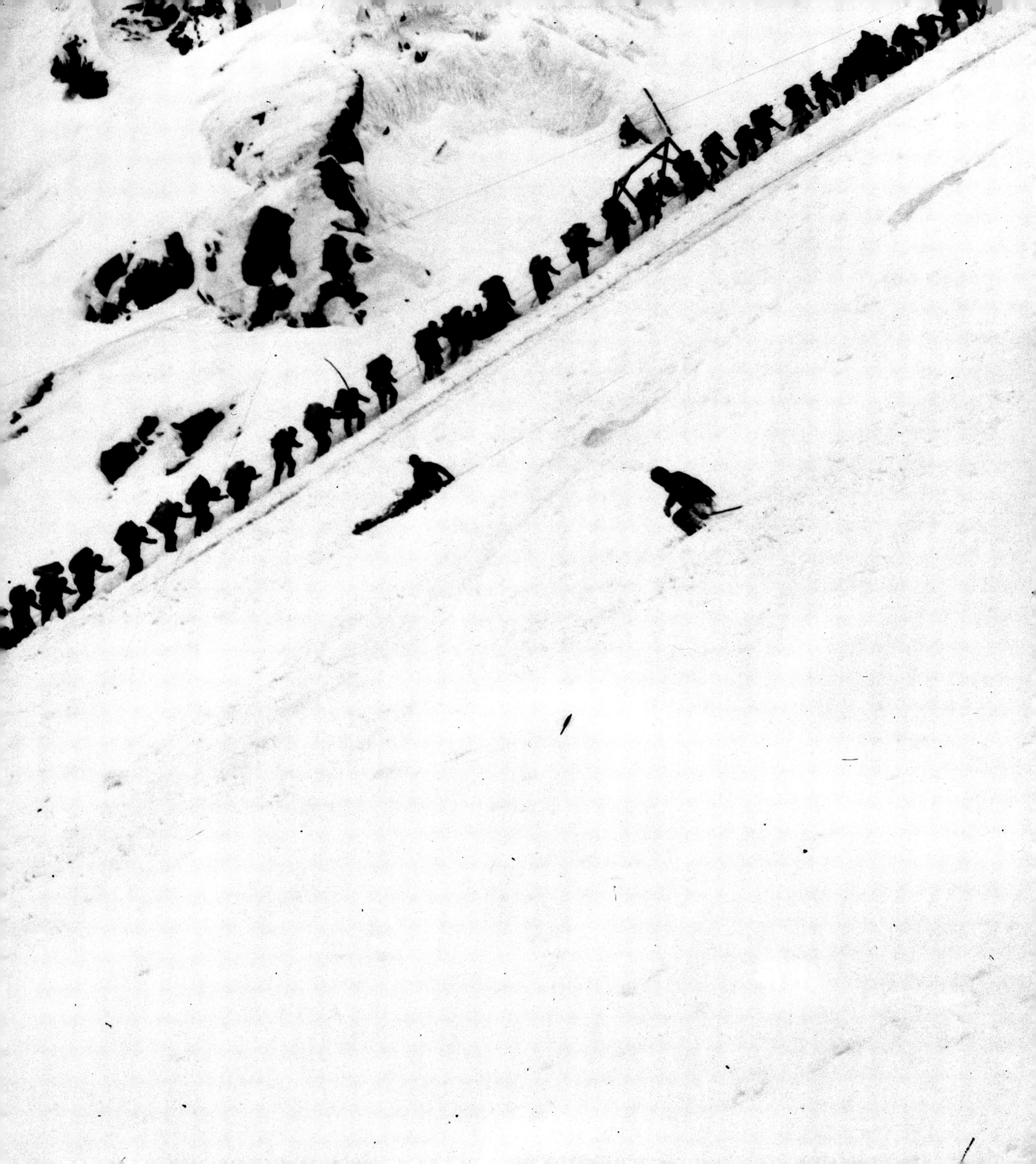

207.   THE LAST CLIMB TO THE SUMMIT OF C⸻OT PASS.   COPYRIGHT 1898.   E.A.Hegg.

Some entrepreneurs built a cable line to winch goods to the top of the pass. Stampeders who couldn't afford it had to backpack.

On Chilkoot Pass

(*Overleaf*) By midwinter, these men had hauled a year's supplies to
the summit. By spring, three dumps were layered in 70 feet of snow.

The Chilkoot look

By the time they reached
the summit of the pass and
deposited their outfits in
a city of supplies, men who
survived the climb – gaunt,
dirty, stinking, exhausted –
bore no resemblance to those
who had been photographed
so cheerfully in the portrait
studios of the Pacific Coast.
These one-time clerks and
office workers were now
seasoned pioneers who had
learned how to load an ox,
to manoeuvre a shoulder pack,
and to protect their eyes
from the glare of the snow,
which, even on dull days,
could make a man blind. In
these photographs, no one is
smiling; indeed, no one is
consciously posing. They look
up for an instant, stare briefly
into the photographer's lens,
then get on with the job.

At the summit of the Chilkoot, a city of supplies

Seventy feet of snow fell on the Chilkoot summit in the winter of 1897-98. The city of supplies shown here, almost devoid of any human presence, was one of two that piled up that winter. Both were buried beneath the snows. Men were often forced to dig for dozens of feet to find their own goods, as the figures at the rear of this scene are doing. Tents, sledges, flour sacks, food cartons all vanished as the snow covered them. Blizzards were some-times so fierce that all movement was halted for a fortnight. When the storm ended, the world atop the pass was pure white – without a hint or sign of the handiwork of man.

With their headquarters shack and customs shed already half hidden in the snow,
the Mounted Police raise the flag to mark the Canadian side of the Chilkoot Pass.

A blizzard strikes and the shack vanishes beneath the drifts as the climbers,
blurred figures in the storm, struggle to remove their outfits before it worsens.

The long, easy slide to the lakes

On the far side of the Coastal Mountains, beyond the fury of the pass and the shrieking gale at the summit, the snow was still blowing, but the trip to the lakes was downhill all the way. With square sails propelling their sleds, the men who had managed to survive the Chilkoot could relax. Ahead lay the frozen shores of Lake Lindemann and beyond that Lake Bennett. The climbing was over. Soon the boat building would begin.

5 The Armada

Down from the coastal mountains the human river flowed, until the lakes that feed the Yukon were humming with activity. By spring, more than thirty thousand men and women were camped for sixty miles along the shores of Lindemann, Bennett, and Tagish, constructing history's strangest armada – seven thousand homemade boats, fashioned from green lumber and designed for a single five-hundred-mile voyage downriver to the golden valleys of the Klondike.

Emerging from the mountains after the long winter's struggle, each man presented a grotesque appearance. Were these skinny scarecrows the same men who had once posed, clear-eyed and confident, in the coastal studios? Their ragged beards and patched clothing made them seem like creatures from some savage and foreign clime, for their faces were smeared with charcoal and their eyes were hidden behind slitted masks to guard against sunburn and snow glare. Gaunt, hard-muscled, and paunchless, they were no longer tenderfeet. Others might have given up, but they were still pushing forward. And now it looked like a boat ride all the way.

Gazing down on the scene spread out before him, each man was faced with a spectacle that caused him to draw breath. On the shores of Lake Bennett the greatest tent city in the world was taking shape. The tents were here by the tens of thousands, every conceivable form of canvas shelter from tiny lean-tos to great circus marquees – tents for every purpose from privy to post office, from chapel to casino. And between the tents, intermingled with the snarl of supplies, sledges, stoves, mining equipment, and tethered animals, were great stacks of timber, mountains of logs, heaps of roughly dressed lumber, and the half-finished skeletons of thousands of boats.

The lakes were a wall of sound. The pounding of thousands of hammers, the screeching of unnumbered whipsaws, the continual crashing of trees (an entire forest was destroyed in a few months) combined with the human and animal cries to shatter the silence of the North.

Welling up within the cacophony was another dissonance: the shrill altercations of embittered partners struggling in the sawpits. After the travail of the passes, life on the lakeshore had promised to be a vacation; now it turned out to be a nightmare. The whipsawing of green lumber was enough to try the patience of a Damon. To transform a freshly cut and peeled log into a series of rough planks required two men – one on the scaffold above, guiding the six-foot saw along a chalk line, the other in the pit below, grasping the handle and pulling downward. As the great hooked teeth bit into the fresh lumber and a spray of sawdust blinded him, the man below swore in a fury at the man above for not guiding the saw, receiving in his turn a tongue-lashing for hanging on too tight. Under this physical and mental strain, friendships snapped, partnerships dissolved, and the most inseparable comrades became the coldest of enemies, dividing up their common gear even to the extent of chopping sacks of flour in two and sawing sledges in half.

Through this leaderless multitude moved the young constables of the North West Mounted Police, acting as arbiters between warring partners and advisers to the amateur boat builders, insisting that a number be painted on each prow and a record kept of all occupants. When the ice broke in the lakes, they were determined to keep a firm hold on the flotilla.

Would the ice never break? By May the snow had gone from the lower slopes, and melt water was gurgling beneath the mosses. The thick ring of boats encircling Bennett was now five deep. The surface was rotting, but the ice still held. The boat builders could only sit and wait.

The outside world was talking of a "stampede" to the Klondike, but the stampeders knew better. Thus far it had been a slow, remorseless struggle. For at least six months they had been members of a frustrating queue that stretched all the way back to the ticket offices of the Pacific Coast. It was the same on the other Trails of '98. On the wet jungle of the Ashcroft trail and the mud of the Stikine, on the glaciers of Alaska's underbelly and the frozen expanse of the lower Yukon, on the banks of the Athabasca, along the Liard and the Mackenzie, the Gravel and the Rat, men were hung up by the forces of climate and geography. Nothing could move. Until the ice melted, the stampede had come to a halt.

Then, on May 29, the ice began to creak. With a low rumble the lakes broke and within forty-eight hours were transformed into water highways of purest glacial green. Out onto the glassy surfaces the outlandish flotilla drifted – 7,124 boats of every description, from kayaks to scows, from canoes to side-wheelers, arks and catamarans, catboats and cockleshells – loaded with thirty million pounds of solid food, a slender breeze filling their sails. The spectacle was unique. As the wind dropped and a golden haze crept over the emerald waters, thousands of ungainly vessels were becalmed beneath the encircling mountains. Nothing like it had been seen before; nothing like it has been seen since.

As they contemplated the scene around them, the men in the boats seemed to sense that they were witnesses to a singular moment in history. Suddenly the fever that had driven them over the passes, the furies that had possessed them in the sawpits, abated. Only a few attempted to paddle fiercely forward. The rest settled back in their crude craft, smoked their pipes, and, as the long June evening merged into twilight, began to sing as they waited for the wind to rise and the sails to carry them down the mountain corridor to the river beyond.

In the vanguard were the eager ones, desperate to be the first across the finish line. Their hopes were soon shattered. Most had never handled a boat before and paid little heed to the roar of tumbling waters ahead. Before they realized it they had plunged into the gloomy gorge of Miles Canyon, a narrow cleft in a wall of basalt with an unholy whirlpool at its centre and beyond that two sets of merciless rapids. One hundred and fifty boats were wrecked and five men lost. As the main flotilla reached this bottleneck, the stampede again ground to a halt.

Now the Mounted Police arrived and provided experienced boatmen to guide the gold seekers through. As each craft emerged from the white water, its occupants were treated to a heart-rending scene on the banks beyond: hundreds of demoralized people, crying and wringing their hands in despair as the remnants of their outfits lay drying out on the bottoms of upturned boats.

Soon the river was speckled with boats for hundreds of miles as the flotilla lost its bunched-up quality. The sun shone without mercy for twenty-two hours a day, blistering the faces of the boatmen while hordes of mosquitoes, gnats, and blackflies drove them to near madness. Those who had not thought to bring netting found it impossible to sleep, and the tensions that had subsided when they embarked on the lakes broke out anew. Comrades who had survived previous quarrels turned against each other. As one wrote, "Brother fought brother and father fought son and the spirit of forbearance and forgiveness was not known on the trail of land and water." At Split-Up Island and Split-Up City men actually chopped frying pans and boats in half rather than compromise. Dawson was only a few hours away; the goldfields were almost within reach. Who needed a partner any longer? Better to dig up the treasure yourself, without help, and keep it all for your own.

In those last few hours, the boatmen travelled without pause, each man taut with tension as the miles glided by. None knew exactly where the town was located, so all hugged the right bank for fear of being swept past. Then, at last, each boat rounded a rocky bluff, and there it was – an incredible miscellany of tents, log cabins, and false-fronted emporiums, all jammed together, stretching for two miles along the bank and spilling over hills, swamp, and river – a weird metropolis mushrooming out of the wilderness a thousand miles from civilization. As each man steered his boat to the shore he must have pinched himself. Was it real? The mists steaming from the marshes in the June sunlight gave the town an eerie look. But it was very real. This was Dawson. This was the goal he had set for himself and after many weary months had achieved. This was the end of the rainbow. This was the city of gold.

The greatest tent city in the world

The Klondike saga is a series of wide-screen spectacles. On the shores of Lake Bennett, once a brooding wilderness, an incredible canvas city sprang up – thousands of tents for every conceivable purpose. The stampeders, more than 20,000 strong, quickly denuded the hills of timber as they struggled to build their strange craft. Yet in a few months this canvas city would vanish.

On the shores of a frozen lake an ungainly armada takes shape

Every style of water craft – catamarans, scows, skiffs, outriggers, junks, kayaks, arks, catboats, and wherries – was fashioned from green lumber on the shores of Bennett and its sister lakes. Some were tiny rafts, little more than three logs hastily bound together; others were shaped like floating packing boxes. There were boats with wedge bottoms, with flat bottoms, with curved bottoms, some circular, others triangular. There were vast 22-ton scows big enough to carry a herd of oxen and great rafts that could be loaded with hay and horses, some of them propelled by sweeps. Others were built from a single log, with a mackinaw coat for a sail. Caulked with spruce pitch and sometimes with underwear, they were constructed for a single journey only. But all had names – *Yellow Garter, Seven-Come-Eleven, Golden Horseshoe* – that hinted, wistfully, at the hopes of those who at great physical and mental cost were preparing for the long race down the river.

Whipsawing

This is the toil that turned the closest friends into the bitterest of enemies–whipsawing green lumber into planks for the crude craft constructed for the river trip. The man below cursed the man above for the cloud of sawdust in his eyes; the man above cursed his mate for hanging on too hard. Two bank clerks, friends from childhood, so inseparable that they married sisters, were driven to such rage that they halved all their goods, even sawing up their flour sacks.

Trees became planks overnight and planks became boats. Mounted Police moved among the builders, cautioning them to "build strong – don't end up in a floating coffin," for most of these men had never built anything in their lives. Now they were constructing a homemade fleet to carry them for five hundred miles down lakes, canyon, rapids, and river. As a precaution each boat had to have a number painted on its prow and check in at the police posts along the route.

Waiting for the ice to break

Spring arrived, water trickled beneath the mosses, and the purple pasque-flower poked its head above the snow patches on the hills, but still the lakes held. The boat builders, oars at the ready, sat and waited, as they had waited at the steamboat docks and at the foot of the passes. The word "stampede" now had a touch of irony to it.

KLONDIKERS EMBARKING AT LAKE BENNETT. June

1898. COPYRIGHT 1898 E.A. Hegg

229

Launching the great flotilla

At last, on May 29, 1898, with a creak and a rumble the rotting ice broke and the great boat race to the Klondike began. On that first day eight hundred craft managed to push off, with every man straining at the oars to try to maintain a lead. Within forty-eight hours the lakes were clear of ice, and a flotilla of 7,124 boats loaded with thirty million pounds of solid food began the long glide to the Klondike. Now, as a young breeze wafted down the alpine corridor, catching the sails, the stampeders settled back in their craft and savoured the experience: the blue slopes perfectly reflected in the mint-green waters, the June sun warming their bones. Again the spectacle was unique: thousands of boats speckling a lake that had, until this year, been as silent as the tomb. Nothing like it had ever been seen before; nothing like it would ever be seen again. The men in the boats began to sing, their voices echoing between the mountains. For a moment the race was forgotten – and so was the grim canyon that lay ahead.

After the canyon, the rapids...

Miles Canyon – "a diminutive Fingal's Cave" its discoverer had called it – was the first obstacle on the voyage. Two sets of rapids followed, and here some inexperienced boatmen foundered. But after that the river trip was a breeze.

...and then clear sailing all the way

6　The Shuffling Throng

The main flotilla reached the Klondike River's mouth on June 8, 1898. From that moment on the boats poured into Dawson day and night without a break for more than a month. Soon there was no space along the shoreline. Later arrivals were forced to tie their craft to other vessels until a phalanx of boats, six deep, stretched for two miles along the waterfront.

As men poured in by the thousands, each with his own soiled and tattered tent, the town ballooned, surging out over the hills and across the two rivers like a great white blossom. Six canvas cities, Dyea and Skagway, Lindemann and Bennett, Tagish and Teslin, had been packed up and brought here to the swampland at the junction of the Klondike and the Yukon rivers.

Although Dawson had been surveyed into a checkerboard pattern, there was nothing tidy about the community the stampeders encountered. Front Street, along the river, was a chaos of sawn lumber, half-finished buildings, and the usual jumble of logs, ladders, and saw horses in a sea of mud. As the first arrivals nosed into the shore, a spring flood that had deluged the town was abating. But Dawson did not dry out until fall. Horses and men thrashed their way through streams of slime or teetered on duckboards half-submerged in the gumbo. On the high boardwalk along the road edge, there was scarcely room to move.

The new arrivals tumbled from the boats, electric with excitement, their energies renewed by the race downriver. And then something odd happened to them. They should, by all evidence, have rushed headlong for the gold creeks, yet thousands did no such thing. Gazing down Front Street at the sawdust, the stumps, and the mud, hearing once more the screech of sawmills and the pounding of hammers, looking up at the hills, white with flapping canvas, and seeing the thousands who had come before them plodding back and forth like sleepwalkers, they became part of an aimless crowd, "curious, listless, dazed, dragging its slow lagging step along the main street."

Of all the bizarre spectacles conjured up by the Klondike phenomenon, this is the strangest. These men had clawed their way north in the face of appalling hazards. Most had been on the trail for the best part of a year, overcoming every natural obstacle in order to reach their goal. But what was that goal? Was it really the rich ground of Eldorado, Bonanza, Last Chance, or Hunker? Thousands did not even trouble to visit the fabled creeks or stake a claim. Others did so perfunctorily, knowing in their hearts that the real ground had long since been taken. Many of these did not bother to sink a shovel into their property. Some, who still clung to the belief that nuggets lay freely about waiting to be scooped up, were finally disillusioned when they realized that the gold lay thirty-odd feet below the valleys and that somebody else had laid claim to it.

Yet disillusionment was not the prime characteristic of the Front Street crowd that summer. Emotional lassitude dominated – after the tensions of the trail, something had snapped. Men wandered about, eyes glazed, like inebriates. All their energies had been funnelled into one driving purpose: to reach the land of gold. Well, they had reached it; and now, in the phrase of the day, they were "used up." For them the adventure was over; there were no more barriers to breach.

And that is the chief explanation for the sudden abatement of the gold fever. Gold had been an excuse. For months they had talked of nothing else. But adventure was what they really hungered for, and that they had achieved. Success was not a sackful of nuggets; it was the satisfaction of having made it. Others had faltered and failed. But they had come through – clerks and salesmen, factory workers and field hands, men who had never carried a pack in their lives or climbed a mountain or built a boat or tested a wild river. They had conquered a wilderness and now, like war veterans, they could join the parade.

Still wearing the faded mackinaws, patched trousers, and high boots of the trail, they plodded up and down Front Street, spectators at the carnival of Dawson, their faces, like their clothes, the colour of dust, their beards left purposely unkempt. Some still wore their fur hats with snow glasses perched on them as a kind of badge. They did not stride; they shuffled, bent slightly forward, unable to erase the posture of the passes.

The real fortune hunters had been more far-sighted. These entrepreneurs had raced into town days ahead of the main flotilla. Their purpose was not to find a gold mine but to find a man who had already found one.

For all of the previous winter Dawson had been a community of millionaires – the early birds who staked the rich ground but whose fortunes could buy nothing. Now the law of supply and demand made healthy profits for those who never bothered to stake a claim. A man who had endured the jeers of his fellows to bring in a scow-load of kittens got an ounce of gold apiece for them from miners starved for companionship. Another sold tinned milk for a dollar a tin; a third made five thousand dollars on women's hats and dresses. An ancient newspaper soaked in bacon grease went for fifteen dollars. A single fresh-laid egg sold for five.

The shuffling throng took its cue from these hucksters. As the river level dropped, a vast bazaar took shape on the wet sandbar along the Dawson waterfront as each man tried to dispose of the ton of goods he had dragged across mountain and canyon. Here you could buy almost anything, often at half the price charged down on the coast. You could get a plug hat, a string of pearls, a pair of satin slippers, a mammoth's tusk, or an entire ox. You could even buy peanuts or pink lemonade.

Gold scales were a drug on the market; every man had brought a set with him to weigh out his fortune. Rifles sold for a dollar because firearms were banned in Dawson: this was not the American frontier. Piles of clothing, washed and rewashed, went for a song. Flour was cheap: each man had packed four hundred pounds over the passes; oatmeal, dried fruit, bacon, and beans sold at sacrifice prices. But few had thought to bring in a broom – these fetched seventeen dollars apiece; and nails, equally scarce, went for eight dollars a pound, for Dawson was in the throes of a building boom. New construction was gobbling up twelve million feet of dressed lumber as fast as a dozen screeching sawmills could turn it out. Lots on the main street sold for twenty thousand dollars. The cheapest single room rented for one hundred dollars a month, almost one hundred times the price of a better room "Outside."

By mid-June the river was alive with steamboats, yellow smokestacks belching white smoke, scarlet paddle wheels churning, pennants fluttering from their masts, decks crowded with dancing girls, gold seekers, businessmen, gamblers – even tourists. By the end of August fifty-six stern-wheelers, eight tugboats, and twenty immense barges had dumped seventy-four hundred tons of freight on Dawson's new docks. You could order oysters on the half shell at the better restaurants, not to mention lobster Newburg and broiled moose chops.

But these luxuries were reserved for the Kings of Eldorado, as the *nouveaux riches* of the Klondike Valley were dubbed. The average stampeder, squatting on Front Street's wooden sidewalk, could only gawk as the famous and infamous were pointed out: Charley Anderson, known as the Lucky Swede because he took a million dollars from a claim foisted on him while he was drunk; or Swiftwater Bill Gates, part-owner of the Monte Carlo Dance Hall, who, it was said, had actually bathed in champagne at Seattle's Rainier-Grand Hotel.

By midsummer, Dawson had mushroomed into the biggest Canadian city west of Winnipeg. Its population ebbed and flowed as boats arrived and left, and as men moved into the hills and back into town. On the trip from the lakes, twenty-eight thousand stampeders had been checked past the Tagish post; another five thousand had come upriver by steamer from Alaska. Dawson had a floating population of at least thirty thousand; by July it boasted two banks, two newspapers, five churches, a telephone service, and a motion picture theatre.

Now the confusion of the trail was transferred to the streets of the new boom town. Dawson changed its shape daily, almost hourly. There were no maps and no street addresses, for tents, cabins, and men were constantly shifting. In this mélange of log and canvas, men circled about, shamefacedly seeking their former partners to make amends for the quarrels in the sawpits and on the river. Often they could not find them. Newcomers vainly sought friends whom they had met on the trail and knew only by their first names. If a man chanced to move his tent he was often lost to his cronies. Spirited off to the hospital, the sick were given up for good. In desperation, people began to post notices on the Alaska Commercial Company's bulletin board offering rewards for information leading to former acquaintances. Front Street was crowded with men trying to find each other or, having made the connection at last, simply squatting on the sidewalk to talk, for there was no other place to go.

By August, the Front Street carnival had reached its zenith, set off against the half-completed backdrop of a dozen saloons, dance halls, and gaming houses. The street was aflutter with banners, pennants, signs, and placards. "GOLD!" the placards screamed. "Gold! Gold! Gold dust bought and sold!" For gold, at sixteen dollars an ounce, was common currency in Dawson.

And again, nothing was quite what it seemed. The gold, frequently salted with brass, iron filings, and sand, was rarely pure. The dance halls, where horns blared and pianos tinkled, were log hovels tarted up with square two-storey fronts. The Oatley Sisters, who sang and danced to a portable organ on a rough platform behind the Bank Saloon, were actually mother and daughter.

It did not matter. When the two women burst into sentimental songs, the crowd fell silent. Many stampeders were three thousand miles from home, some as much as ten thousand. If they had received any mail at all – waiting for hours in another queue as they had waited at the passes and the lakes – the letters were months old. Now, as the bell-like voices began to pipe out the familiar songs – "Break the News to Mother," "A Bird in a Gilded Cage" – each man was alone with his thoughts. Those who had funds could scramble up on the platform and, for a dollar, dance three rounds with one of the women. The others could only watch wistfully and think back on the crowded events of the gold-rush year and the families they had left behind.

By late August, when the birches and aspens grew sere on the hills and the first touch of frost sent a chill across the tent town, it was time for decision. A third of those who had poured into Dawson in June and July bought a steamboat ticket and left the Klondike forever. The rest decided to tough it out. Those who still had most of their ton of supplies built log cabins and settled down for the winter. Some took odd jobs in Dawson to tide them over to spring. Hundreds more decided to venture out to the creeks where, they had once been told, the gold lay thickly on the ground waiting to be shovelled into gunny sacks. They were wiser now; was it only a year since those tales had beguiled them? Out they trudged along the Klondike River road to Bonanza and Eldorado, to Hunker and Last Chance, and over the divide to Sulphur and Dominion – not to stake a claim and dig for gold but to toil for those who had long since struck it rich. It was backbreaking work, but, after a year of questing, they were well prepared.

Scene along waterfront of Dawson
Spring of 1898

~ En route to Klondike Gold Fields ~

620
Copyrighted
M.H. CRAIG DAWSON

The first view of Dawson City

This is the spectacle that greeted the stampeders as they rounded the Yukon bluff and saw, spread out before them, the city of their dreams. In the foreground is Klondike City, better known as Lousetown. Beyond the mouth of the Klondike is Dawson proper–a jumble of tents, warehouses, mud, and new lumber. The hedgerow of boats tied up along the shore would soon stretch six deep for two miles as twenty thousand men poured into town to join the shuffling throng.

742. DAWSON CITY N.W.T. COPYRIGHT 1898 C.A. Hegg

Burgeoning Dawson, seen from the opposite end of town. Built on a frozen swamp, the town was flooded that spring when an ice jam caused the Yukon to rise over these flats. Within a year, the empty spaces were covered with tents, warehouses, theatres, and cabins. By autumn even the hills were white with canvas. In the distance we can just see the Klondike's mouth.

Front Street, still stump-obstructed, ran along the waterfront where the first arrivals, unable to find quarters, lived on their boats. Soon this would not be possible. The water fell, exposing a vast sandbar, and new warehouses and docks sprang up. Already, in the middle distance, a banner advertising the Criterion theatre can be seen. The carnival is about to start.

Nothing to do; nowhere to go

Here is the most puzzling spectacle of the Klondike stampede: thousands of gold seekers milling about, squatting on piles of fresh lumber, shuffling up and down Front Street in an aimless parade. For nine months these men have been struggling against terrible odds to reach the goldfields, but now thousands have not even bothered to look for gold. Why? Is it because the early birds have staked the richest ground? Or is it that their real goal was not the treasure beneath the Klondike valleys but the Klondike itself? These are the survivors, the men who have made it over the passes and down the lakes. For them it seems to have been enough.

Mud and boredom

What to do in Dawson? What to do if all your funds were tied up in the outfit you had bought with your savings in those manic days when the Klondike fever raged across a continent? Dawson's streets were not paved with gold but covered in a thick chowder of muck. Horses could scarcely make it down these rivers of slime. Men stood around in knee-length rubber boots wondering what to do – to sell what they had for passage home? Or to take part in the continuing adventure of the great stampede?

Bowery Street, Dawson.

When the river level dropped, a vast bazaar sprang up on the sandbar that lay exposed in front of Dawson. Here disillusioned men put their outfits on the market and prepared to take a steamboat home. Beyond those emaciated horses in the foreground of Bowery Street, stalls and tents push everything from rifles to logs for cabins. Since firearms were banned by the police, guns sold cheaply. But everything – tinned goods, snowshoes, picks, axes, stoves, and flour sacks – had its price.

Boats became temporary shops as the newcomers hawked everything from stoves to long johns.

46068
ASAHEL CURTIS
COPYRIGHTED
1898

Its weight in gold

Freshly baked bread was a delicacy for men who had lived on hard tack for the best part of a year. In Dawson, gold was legal tender, and no emporium, even this modest open-air bakery, could operate without a set of delicately balanced scales. The gold was rarely pure, being laced with black sand and iron filings; known as commercial dust, it was universally discounted. Compared with fresh bread, the tinned goods and dried foods brought in over the passes sold for little. Fresh onions were so scarce they sold in drugstores as scurvy cures at two dollars each.

Paying through the nose

Dawson's prices were the highest on the continent, as these photographs demonstrate. On the Outside, as the rest of the world was called, a shave and a haircut went for the traditional "two bits," or 25 cents; here it cost a dollar and a quarter. You could get waffles and coffee or a glass of cold lemonade for a nickel anywhere in North America except here, where freight rates were sky high. With the sun shining 22 hours a day, these emporiums never closed. A man could stagger out of the Pavilion at 4 a.m. and spend his last quarter on a waffle fresh from the griddle.

The false fronts of Dawson

In the summer of 1898 Dawson was a hastily thrown together city of logs and crude lumber. Buildings went up overnight as the sawmills, working 24 hours a day, turned out millions of board feet of planking. The names of the dance halls, hotels, and gaming houses were far more pretentious than their architecture. But they all made money.

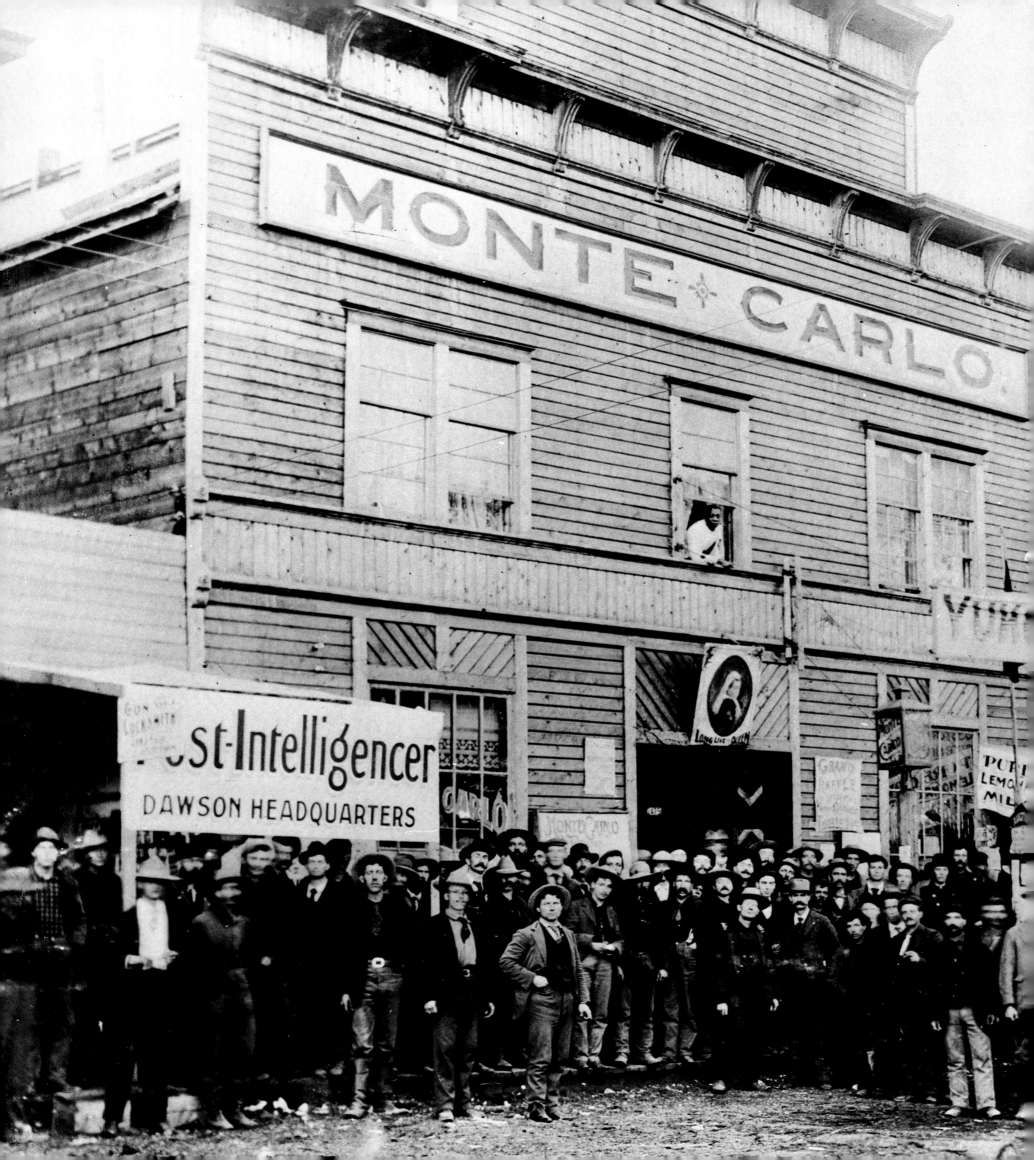

The famous Monte Carlo

This was Dawson's best-known palace of pleasure. Like most other emporiums on Front Street, it was constantly changing hands. The notorious Swiftwater Bill Gates was one of the early owners. His partner foolishly dispatched him to Seattle to purchase ten-foot mirrors, velvet carpets, oil paintings, and ten thousand dollars' worth of fixtures, but Swiftwater spent the money on wine and women. A later owner, Ed Holden, lost it to Kid Kelly in a faro game. The original building, shown here, was decidedly unglamorous. It housed an unprepossessing saloon (shown overleaf), a dark little gaming room, and behind that a small, Spartan theatre with hard benches.

Queuing up...

The queues stretched for blocks as hundreds waited for their mail or tried to record claims or buy miners' licences. Some took advantage of the "five-dollar door" at the gold office, where faster service could be purchased for the usual bribe.

...for mangled mail

Men stood for as long as three days to get their mail – or paid five dollars to a woman to hold their place. One steamboat dumped 5,700 letters into town, some so badly mauled the envelopes were missing. One letter arrived dated June, 1894.

On Dawson's docks, 7,400 tons of freight

By the end of August, 1898, fifty-six stern-wheelers had dumped 7,400 tons of freight onto the newly constructed wharfs along Dawson's Front Street. As early as July 1 the new San Francisco chef at the Regina Café could feature on his Dominion Day menu such luxury items as "Rock Point oysters, lobster Newburg, and chicken salad *en mayonnaise*." Many of these river steamers were equally opulent, with palatial dining rooms of mahogany, staterooms equipped with two or three berths and monogrammed bed linen, and afternoon tea served from pots of sterling silver. The boats ran on birchwood cut along the river. The *Yukoner*'s captain, the dashing John Irving, invited the woodcutters aboard for a round of champagne while a band on the deck played furiously and a bevy of dancing girls cavorted. The biggest cargo of all was liquor. In a single season, this fleet of boats brought in 120,000 gallons.

153

7   The Creeks

Before George Carmack and his Indian companions made the famous strike on Bonanza Creek on August 16, 1896, the valleys of the Klondike watershed were no different from thousands of others that grooved and pitted the Yukon interior plateau. Unmarred by the glacial advance that tore up so much of the North (there was not enough moisture in the Yukon interior to support an ice age), they were the products of an erosion pattern millions of years old. Deep, mile-wide valleys these, terraced by bench land that hinted at ancient upheavals in the earth's crust. Far below in the bottoms, meandering through the mosses and willows and over the chalky gravels, blue-white creeks gurgled and glittered.

There was no mother lode in the Klondike, though many sought it – no thick vein of hard-rock gold hidden in the bowels of King Solomon's Dome, from which the richest creeks radiated. That had long since been ground to nuggets and dust by the same erosive action that gouged out the valleys. "Moose pastures," the early prospectors dubbed these with a sneer. Perhaps that is why it was a squaw man, not a prospector, who stumbled on the first nugget.

Far beneath the floors of these pastures and high up on the benches, caught in the flaky bedrock of subterranean stream beds long since gone dry, lay the richest gravels in the world. To find those ancient watercourses – the pay-streak, to use the colloquial phrase – thousands of men were ripping the valleys apart, driving shaft after questing shaft thirty feet or more below the surface, stripping all moss and plant life from the valley floor, denuding the slopes of birch, aspen, and spruce, and pumping millions of gallons of water down sluice boxes to wash the gold from the pay dirt.

The newcomers venturing out for the first time to the goldfields were treated to another of those extraordinary spectacles that punctuate the gold-rush saga. From rim to rim, the great valleys and clefts of the Klondike watershed buzzed with activity. The once verdant floors were now glistening deserts of black mud. Mountains of gravel, thrown up from the bench diggings, stained the slopes white. Flumes and sluice boxes fingered their way between hundreds of log cabins strewn helter-skelter from creek mouth to canyon. The landscape was a litter of rockers and boilers, steam engines and pumps, hoses and winches, trestles and rail lines.

Only now did the late arrivals comprehend the effort required to wrest the treasure from the grip of the bedrock. To find the gold, to bring it to the surface and wash it out could require the better part of a year's work. First, each man must locate the pay-streak that he hoped wriggled somewhere beneath his claim–none knew exactly where. To do that he must burn his way down through the permafrost with wood fires, a foot at a time, shovelling away the thawed muck until he finally reached bedrock. If the bedrock failed to yield any gold, he started again–and again, if necessary –until he found what he was seeking. Then he must tunnel laterally through the permafrost, following the old stream bed and winching the pay dirt to the top of the shaft, a bucket at a time.

To do that, he needed hired help. And so the newcomers, who had thought of "digging" for gold in terms of digging for potatoes, found themselves squeezed into the bowels of the earth, working for wages, choking and gasping in the smoky shafts, shivering from the marrow-chilling cold of the frozen clay, and hacking away at the granite-hard permafrost day after day, week after week, while above them the fog of winter crept across the valley. At night they slept in candlelit hovels of rough logs almost as murky and as suffocating as the shafts, and fetid with the stench of undergarments drying over red-hot stoves.

Nor did the spring bring relief, for now the labourers, emerging like insects from the shafts, blinking in the new sunlight, were put to work shovelling gravel from the dumps of pay dirt into the sluice boxes. Hour after hour they toiled until each shovelful seemed to hold a hundredweight while backs and shoulders cried out in protest. At the end of each three-day period another ordeal faced them. The water was turned off, the matting in the bottom of the sluice lifted, and the gold panned out by hand. All day long they squatted on their haunches, doubled over the pan, hands half-frozen by the icy water, arms and shoulders working ceaselessly as, ounce by ounce, they washed out another man's gold. Over and over the process was repeated–shovelling and panning, panning and shovelling–until all the pay dirt hauled up during the winter months was washed away.

Their spare hours were few, for the season was short and the water precious. It was brought to the sluice boxes and rockers, sometimes from miles away, by hand-dug ditches and wooden flumes. By midsummer, when the snow had left the hills, the flow was reduced to a trickle.

At the junction of Bonanza and Eldorado, not far from Carmack's original discovery claim, the work reached a fever pitch. Eldorado, the richest creek in the Klondike with thirty claims each worth an initial million, poured directly into Bonanza at *its* richest corner. High above the confluence of the two creeks were three golden benches: French Hill, Cheechako Hill, and Gold Hill, in whose depths the famous "white channel," an ancient alluvial stream course loaded with dust, snaked and twisted. The gully between French Hill and Cheechako Hill was called Big Skookum Gulch, and at its mouth was the richest single sliver of land in history, the famous Dick Lowe Fraction, a pie-shaped wedge just eighty-six feet wide at its broadest point. Accidentally created by imperfect staking, it was reluctantly claimed by an ex-muleskinner who took half a million from it. Now the gaping crowd of toilers could spy Dick Lowe himself, roaring drunk, driving his spanking team up the valley road, a dance hall girl beside him, or, of an evening, elbowing his way to the bar of Max Endleman's Gold Hill Hotel in Grand Forks to order drinks for the multitude.

Grand Forks, the largest town in the Yukon next to Dawson, had a floating population of five thousand. Its social élite, the Eldorado Kings, had been penniless two years before. Now, to the new boys, the names of these instant millionaires were magic. Clarence Berry of Number 5 Eldorado had so much gold that, it was said, he kept a coal-oil can full of it near his front door with a sign reading "Help Yourself." His partner, an Austrian immigrant named Antone Stander, had just stolen Max Endleman's girl friend with a gift of a diamond necklace, twenty thousand dollars in dust, a lard pail full of nuggets, and a living allowance of a thousand dollars a month. Arkansas Jim Hall got off cheaper; he bought himself a wife for twenty thousand dollars and no extras.

It was the stories – all true – of the unbelievable wealth of these and other men that had touched off the stampede. Now they stood at the bar of the Magnet or the Gold Hill guzzling champagne at thirty dollars a bottle, squeezing the plump arms of the latest dance hall beauty, and squandering their fortunes. In the background, the veterans of the passes, soiled, shabby, and exhausted, could only stand and marvel as they might marvel at royalty and wish that somehow, somewhere, they, too, might someday strike it rich.

Golden Eldorado

This was the richest creek in the Klondike watershed with at least 30 claims worth an initial million dollars each.

362-a
H&S

The Diggings

Placer gold – the only kind found in the Klondike – cannot be mined without water. Nor can it be taken from the Arctic earth until the permafrost above the pay-streak has been thawed all the way to bedrock. Thus, the valleys of the Yukon were soon denuded of timber. The hills were marked by long ditches bringing water, often from miles away, to the wooden flumes snaking along the valley floor and to the sluice boxes that pointed, like skeletal fingers, to each man's dump of pay dirt. These incredibly rich piles had been winched up from the bottom of each shaft during the winter. Now men worked hour after hour without a break, shovelling the dirt into the rushing waters of the sluice. Here the gravel and clay were washed away but the heavier gold remained, caught in the riffles and matting of the box as it had once been caught in the grooves of the flaky bedrock. Three times a week the water was turned off, the matting lifted, and the gold panned out – another backbreaking job for those who had once expected to dig it out by the shovelful as easily as working a vegetable garden. Now, standing or squatting in icy water, bespattered with mud, clay, and slime, they toiled from dawn to dusk with shovel and pan, helping to dig out another man's gold.

Treasure on the benches

High above the golden valleys, the bench land – unknown to the early prospectors – held a fortune in nuggets. This was the site of another ancient stream course, which had flowed through the Klondike region before millions of years of erosion gouged out the great valleys. The first miners sneered at the tenderfeet who sank shafts in the hillsides, but the jeers subsided when the famous White Channel was discovered – a twisting course of blanched gravel that cut directly across Bonanza Creek near its junction with Eldorado. Soon the flanks of the Bonanza Valley were stained white as men with rockers literally shook the gold free from the dross, sifting it through a wire mesh sieve and into the sluices. This is Gold Hill. Grand Forks lies just below.

The richest ground in history

The men posing with picks in their hands on the previous page are standing on some of the richest ground in the Klondike –Clarence Berry's Claim No. 5 on Eldorado Creek. Directly opposite the Berry claim were the three richest benches – French Hill, Gold Hill, and Cheechako Hill, shown at the right. The Klondike did not produce as much gold as South Africa or Australia, but it was unique in the richness of its most famous claims. A rope with a plumb bob marked the boundary of some claims where the gold lay thickest: a few inches either way could mean a loss of thousands. Berry, a penniless farmer from California, was tending bar at Fortymile in 1896 and so was among the first to learn of the Klondike strike. With the gold he dug up on his own he was able to employ scores of men, like the ones shown here. Berry was one of the few Klondike "Kings" who kept their millions. His partner, Antone Stander, split the profits and spent all of his on wine and women in the saloons of Grand Forks.

33

LARSS & DUCLOS
PHO-
DAWSON Y.T

The Klondike look

Here are the faces of the survivors – the men who made it all the way
to the gold diggings. Tough, lean, and hardy, they have in one year learned
enough about life to face any vicissitude with boldness and resilience.

Above the shaft

At the head of the shaft on Claim
No. 44 Below, Bonanza Creek, two
women join the men for a group
photograph. Claims were numbered
Above and Below Discovery, which
means that this 500-foot claim was
about four miles downstream from
George Carmack's original find.
The winch in the background leads
down to the bedrock at the bottom
of the shaft, where these men,
toiling on their knees, chip away at
the pay-streak with picks and shovels,
sending the results upward by
bucket. *(Overleaf)* These shafts were
thawed out from the permanently
frozen clays and silts. Some went as
deep as thirty feet but did not have
to be cribbed because their frozen
sides remained as hard as granite.

Housekeeping on the creeks

The men on the creeks lived where they worked, in tents or in log hovels chinked with moss and with the same mud churned up by the eager search for gold. Shafts, sluice boxes, and dumps of pay dirt lay cheek by jowl with primitive living quarters. Men lived on beans and salt pork and usually slept in the mud-spattered clothes in which they toiled. Laundry was expensive, but there was little time in which to wash your own underwear and little space for it to dry. Klondike millionaires lived no better, but at least were able to afford a binge at the Gold Hill Hotel.

MARY'S HOTEL

NO 20 BELOW ON BONANZA

DAWSON. Y.T.

None of the glamour of the goldfields (to be copied and distorted in half a hundred "Klondike nights" in the century that followed) can be discerned here. The hovel above, constructed from green logs and mud, is actually a hotel. In summer the roofs of these shacks were bright with wild flowers – welcome relief from the drabness of the mud flats.

INTERIOR 16 MILE ROADHOUSE YUKON RIVER

The interior of a Klondike roadhouse. Seated on bunks and benches around the ubiquitous Yukon stove, men read by a coal-oil lamp, clean their weapons, pet their huskies beneath an overhead jungle of steaming underwear and boots. Sealed airtight against the bone-chilling cold outside, these rooms were stifling – and pungent with the stench of human sweat.

By candlelight men tested the pay dirt in the comfort of a cluttered cabin. Only when the gold was melted into bars and weighed did they know the dimensions of their fortune.

City of Gold

For those who came and stayed for a year, the Klondike was a theatrical experience, perhaps the greatest of their lives. Long after the horrors of the trail had been diminished by time's inverted telescope, the veterans of the stampede would remember with crystal clarity the spectacle of nine-year-old Margie Newman standing heel-deep in nuggets on the stage of the Monte Carlo; or Cad Wilson warbling her famous signature song, "Such a Nice Girl, Too"; or Frank Slavin, the Sydney Cornstalk, boxing Joe Boyle in a fight promoted by young Tex Rickard; or Captain Jack Crawford, the "Poet Scout," in buckskins and Stetson dispensing ice cream from his hovel, The Wigwam; or Silent Sam Bonnifield, raking in a poker pot of $150,000 at the Bank Saloon without cracking a smile.

Dawson City ran on gold. Those who had it spent it; those who didn't watched the town's élite fling their fortunes away. They watched Roddy Conners, a thickset little Irishman, squander fifty thousand dollars at a dollar a dance, capering about the floor with two sisters, Jacqueline and Rosalinde, better known as Vaseline and Glycerine. They watched Phantom Archibald drink himself into poverty at a cost of twenty-five thousand dollars. They watched Ed Holden lose the Monte Carlo to Kid Kelly on the turn of a card. They watched one man pay a waiter to fill a tub with wine at twenty dollars a bottle so that Cad Wilson could take a bath in it. They watched the manager of the Alaska Commercial lose everything he owned and his job as well on the turn of the wheel at the Opera House.

Once they had all hungered for gold. Now it seemed the cheapest of trifles, treated almost with contempt by those who had struck it rich. Big Alex McDonald, the "King of the Klondike," once invited a lady reporter to help herself from a bowl containing forty-five pounds of nuggets. "They mean nothing to me," he said. "Take as many as you please. There are lots more."

"Expense!" expostulated Pat Galvin, the Bonanza millionaire, when his nephew urged financial caution. "Don't show your ignorance by using that cheap Outside word. We don't use it here. Never repeat it in my presence again.... That word is not understood in the North. If you have money, spend it; that's what it's for and that's the way we do business." By the spring of 1899 Pat Galvin had spent it all.

For gold was not the most precious commodity in Dawson that year, as Wilson Mizner, a local *bon vivant* discovered. He held up a restaurant hoping to get enough chocolates to turn the head of his sweetheart, Nellie the Pig. Alas for Mizner; gold could be had for the reaching, but the chocolates were locked away in the restaurant's safe.

Many a stampeder, standing at the bar of the Tivoli, the Combination, or the Palace Grand must have marvelled at this conspicuous consumption. High above him in the private boxes he could spy the Eldorado Kings buying champagne at sixty dollars a quart for women with names like the Oregon Mare, Sweet Marie, or Flossie de Atley, the Girl with the Baby Stare. One man squandered seventeen hundred dollars in a single night in this fashion. *Why?* the cheechakos asked themselves; but then they were faced with a second question: *How would we behave in similar circumstances?* Would they, too, not wish to be suspended above the sweaty, turbulent crowd, publicly indulging in the gratification of the flesh? What was the difference between a private box in the Monte Carlo and a private box in New York's opera house?

In 1899, as the Dawson carnival reached its zenith, Thorstein Veblen published his famous critique of the leisure class. Certainly, Veblen's "conspicuous waste" applied to the moneyed élite of the city of gold. What a private railroad car was to a Morgan or a Vanderbilt a $2,500 team of matched huskies was to a Nigger Jim Daugherty or a Coatless Curly Munro. Daugherty even had a built-in bar on his sled. Munro spent $4,320 on dogfood for six puppies. Clarence Berry laid out $400 a ton for hay to feed the only Jersey cow in town. What was gold for if you could not use it to impress the world? If you could not build a fine brownstone mansion on Front Street you could certainly buy a dance hall, the quintessential status symbol. Half a dozen mining kings did just that. To be pointed out on the street, to be gawked at in your own dance palace, to be whispered about, to be known as a Somebody when, just two years before, you had been a nobody–that was what the Klondike aristocracy craved, and that was what gold would buy. In Dawson men lived for the day, as men do in wartime. As Diamond-Tooth Gertie put it, "The poor ginks have just got to spend it, they're that scared they'll die before they have it all out of the ground."

It was hard not to catch the spending fever, even if you had little to spend. If you could not afford to buy a dance hall girl for her weight in gold, as Chris Johansen of Whiskey Hill had done, you could at least grasp one around the waist for a dollar and whirl her about the tiny floor for a single lap. For a few dollars more you could step around the corner to the cribs of Paradise Alley and rent yourself a partner for an hour or a night. Everything was for sale or rent in Dawson: the women who ran the bawdy cigar stores offered more than tobacco.

And yet, in the midst of all this wealth, a niggardly town council refused to raise the wages of the local firefighters. It was a costly error. With the firemen on strike and the boilers cold, a tongue of flame shot up from the bedroom of a dance hall girl on the second floor of the Bodega Saloon. The date was April 26, 1899. Within minutes the core of the town was a sheet of flame.

With the temperature hugging forty-five below, half of Front Street was ablaze. In the stillness of that night, the flames leaped vertically in long tongues, vaporizing moisture into clouds of steam that enveloped the town. Hogsheads of liquor burst open, the whiskey freezing as it ran into the streets. As the saloons and dance halls began to collapse, Paradise Alley caught fire, and the women ran naked and screaming into the icy lane.

Nothing, it seemed, could quench the inferno. The water froze in the hoses before it reached the nozzles, ripping the canvas to shreds. Even dynamite could not stop the conflagration. The town's most notorious structures – one hundred and seventeen buildings in all – were reduced to charcoal. "Well," said Walter Washburn, as he watched his Opera House crumble, "that's the way I made it and that's the way it's gone. So what the hell!"

Even as he spoke, the vault inside the Bank of British North America burst open, spewing out its contents – dust and nuggets, gold watches, jewelled stickpins and bracelets – the loot of the Klondike now fused into one molten mass, mingling with the steaming clay.

A sturdier town rose from the ashes – a town of plate glass windows and carpeted floors, of Turkish baths and linen napery, of silver and crystal, grand pianos, electricity. Yet, though few sensed it, Dawson had already passed its peak. The last stragglers, arriving gaunt and hollow-eyed after two dreadful years on the so-called all-Canadian trails out of Edmonton, caught the feeling of anticlimax. Thousands still walked the streets seeking work, but there was less and less work. In the outside world the fever had passed; "Klondike" had become an expression of contempt; gold pans sold as dishpans at a fraction of their value.

And then a familiar tingle rippled through the community. Something was in the wind again – but what? Two thousand miles downriver something electric had happened. Was it true? Nobody could be sure, but as the rumours grew, men began to trickle out of town.

By midsummer the news was confirmed. A fortune in gold had been discovered on the beaches of Nome, Alaska. The sands were staked for miles; saloons were opening; money was changing hands; millions, it was said, could be had for the digging. In a single month Dawson was drained. Steamboats heading downriver were jammed with passengers. Saloons emptied, real estate values dropped, dance halls lost their customers. In a single week in August, eight thousand people left Dawson forever. The Klondike quest was over, but, like the continuous film show in the Criterion movie house, another had begun.

DIME
MRS McDONALD
FANCY DRESS MAKING
AND LADIES TAILORING.
LAUNDRY
BROS
AND
WHOLESALE & RETAIL.
H. B. FOLEY
CIGARS

FRONT ST. DAWSON Y.T.

Dawson grows up

By the spring of 1899, Front Street had already changed its shape, with new theatres, saloons, and gaming houses springing up like mushrooms. The town was still chaotic – dogs dragged their burdened sledges through frozen mud, firewood was heaped helter-skelter in the roadway, a potpourri of signs and banners vied with each other. Here, four thousand miles from civilization, surrounded by hundreds of thousands of square miles of wilderness, "the San Francisco of the North" lived up to its name – livelier, richer, and better equipped than many Canadian and American communities. Dawson had telephone service, running water, steam heat, electricity, and even motion pictures. It covered several square miles, spilled across two rivers, and crawled up the surrounding hills; but its pulse beat swiftest here, on dance hall row. Front Street was lively but also unstable. Its buildings were constantly burning down and being rebuilt, switching ownership. Sometimes shops changed both name and locale, so that the street was never the same from month to month. Yet in one sense it never changed: to walk into one building was to walk into all. Behind the ornate façades were dingy, ridged-roof buildings of logs or green lumber. Dawson that spring was an illusion. But then, it was fashioned on fantasy.

The gold moves in

Tightly packed in long pokes of caribou hide, guarded by a special detachment of soldiers, gold by the wagonload rolls in from the creeks to the bank in Dawson. In this cart there is $400,000 worth of treasure, priced at $16 a Troy ounce. In 1983 the value would be almost twelve million. The soldiers here are members of the Yukon Field Force, a special detachment made up of officers and men from the Royal Canadian Rifles, the Royal Canadian Dragoons, and the Royal Canadian Artillery, sent north to reinforce the Mounted Police by a government concerned that the concentration of Americans in the Yukon (its boundaries still in dispute) might cause an insurrection that would lose the territory to Alaska and the United States.

The gold moves out

Men in wing collars, with diamond stickpins in their foulards, ran the roulette wheels and faro tables, where the Klondike Kings were easily separated from their hoards. Gambling was legal in Dawson (it still is), but the Mounted Policeman seen here will make sure the wheel is honest and that at midnight on Saturday the house will shut tight to mark the Lord's Day.

Law and order

In their dress uniforms, the officers of the North West Mounted Police look suitably correct. Actually, the law was lenient in Dawson. No one could pack a gun, but in the cribs of Paradise Alley, which ran directly behind Front Street, the prostitutes plied their trade openly. These are sturdy young women – they had to be, to make it all the way to Dawson.

Paradise Alley

There were seventy cribs on the famous alley – a double line of log and frame shacks, each with a girl's name painted over the doorway. Here, fat Belgian girls in shapeless garments plied their trade for the profit of the sleek little pimps or *maques* who had brought them across the Chilkoot and to whom they were now in bondage – white slaves in the literal sense. The women who ran the "bawdy cigar stores" were a cut above these, but they sold much more than tobacco.

Queens
of the
dance halls

For every gaming room there was also a theatre-cum-dance hall, a device to lure the customers to the faro tables. Most of the actresses who played in *Camille* or *Uncle Tom's Cabin* or the vaudeville turns that followed came down from the stage when the shows ended at midnight. When the pit was cleared of benches and the band struck up, they took the paying customers out onto the floor for that "long dreamy juicy waltz." For one circuit of the small room each miner paid a dollar; his partner received a percentage of the take. Her main object, however, was to lure her man into one of the private boxes, where champagne was dispensed at thirty dollars a pint. These women were not prostitutes; they picked their men carefully, choosing either wealthy miners or members of the gambling fraternity. At least one, Cécile Marion, was auctioned off for her weight in gold.

Larss&Duclos
Dawson.

Front Street in flames...

The date is April 26, 1899; the time: early morning.
A dance hall girl has dropped a lamp, and Dawson's flimsy buildings are tinder. On that night, the firemen were on strike, the boilers cold, the temperature 45 below. Fires had to be set to thaw the frozen surface of the river so that water could be pumped to the scene. By then half of Front Street was in flames. It was so cold that men in furs could not feel the blast of heat that caused clouds of steam to condense into an icy fog. Finally, as the crowd groaned in despair, blasting powder was used to blow up buildings in the path of the fire.

...Dawson in ashes

Half of Dawson was destroyed in the holocaust.
Men offered thousands to anyone who could save their buildings, in vain.
Every saloon, gaming house and dance hall between the Monte Carlo (scorched but not destroyed) and Belinda Mulroney's famous Fairview Hotel (completely draped in mud-soaked blankets) was totally destroyed. Caught between river and swamp, the fire burned itself out but left, of all things, several shapeless piles of ice blocks, cut for summertime use and covered with sawdust as insulation. Ironically, they alone had survived heat so intense it even melted the gold in the bank.

Reviewing
the damage

Front Street was a shambles and Dawson was exhausted. In the lobby of the blanket-draped Fairview, scores of homeless men and women slept in two-hour shifts, then walked down to look at the smoking ruin that marked the old business section of the town. The Pioneer Saloon was gone; so were the Northern, the Tivoli, the Aurora, and the Opera House – 117 buildings in all consumed by the flames. The loss was reckoned at a million dollars, and it all could have been avoided had the town's council met the firemen's demands for higher pay. In a city of millionaires, a penny-pinching administration had brought about a tragedy.

Dawson rebuilds

Within twelve hours after his saloon – the oldest in Dawson –
was destroyed, Tom Chisholm had opened a new Aurora in a
tent and was doing business again. In spite of high prices
(nails sold for 25 cents apiece) the town began to rebuild. On
the faces of its people was a grim determination to look
ahead. For by now they had learned how to conquer despair.

Up from the ashes

The new Dawson was a much more sophisticated town.
On Front Street the architecture took on some of the frontier
flamboyance associated with the late-Victorian age. All these
buildings were constructed in just two months following the fire.
Then, on July 4, this predominantly American town celebrated.

Arizona Charlie opens the Palace Grand

The Palace Grand Dance Hall fitted Dawson's new sophistication. The mahogany bar, enriched by massive oil paintings and patronized by men in wing collars and Homburgs, is a far cry from the crowded saloon of the Monte Carlo, shown on pages 148-149. Advertised as the most lavish establishment in the North, it was constructed from the remains of two steamboats. When it opened, the proprietor held a banquet for forty persons and placed a hundred-dollar bill beneath each plate. Charlie Meadows, seen at the centre of the photograph, was a former western scout and sharpshooter whose family had been wiped out by Apaches and who boasted he had fought hand to hand with Geronimo. A veteran of the Buffalo Bill and Pawnee Bill Wild West shows, he could shoot the spots off a playing card at thirty feet. In his new dance hall he performed by shooting glass balls held between his wife's thumb and forefinger. One day he shot off her thumb, and the exhibitions ceased. The building still stands in Dawson, restored in the early 1960s. The lobby bar had long since vanished, but its position was determined when a bar-shaped line of gold was panned out from beneath the floor boards. It had lain there for sixty years, having drifted down from the pokes of the customers of 1899.

Dawson's high society

Cad Wilson, Dawson's best-known performer, could afford
a black butler and champagne, for she drew the highest salary of
anyone on the stage. She got by on personality, not looks.
Men used to toss gold nuggets to her when she sang and danced.
The boys in the backroom, it turns out, were real.

Steele of
the Mounted
takes his ease

Dawson's leading citizen, its father figure and arbiter, is photographed at midnight, out of uniform *(extreme left)*. "The Lion of the Yukon" was perhaps the most popular man in Dawson, which he administered with an iron but fair hand. Having shepherded the armada of homemade boats down the Yukon, Steele arrived in Dawson with orders to keep the peace. That he did. Dawson ran wide open, but Steele allowed no hand guns, no disorderly conduct, no obscenity, no cheating, no risqué theatrical performances, no sedition on the stage, and no labour on the Lord's Day. He imposed two punishments only, the milder a stint at hard labour on the police woodpile. The tougher was a blue ticket to leave town – simple banishment from the goldfields that so many had tried so hard to reach. Sam Steele's rough justice worked. In 1898 there was no murder in Dawson and no major theft. The phrase "Steele of the Mounted" went into the language and was used as both a book title and a film title. It was very much a case of the name fitting the man.

PHOTOGRAPHED
AT MIDNIGHT DAWSON JUNE 99

In the city of gold, a new sophistication

By 1899, a young new élite had begun to appear in what had been a rough,
tough, all-male mining camp. Clothes became smarter, "respectable" women
arrived, and the young bloods took up sports and formed hiking clubs.

WANTE
Quartz Place
BY
A.J.BANNERM
MINE BRO
GENERAL A

POST OFFICE

WAITING FOR MAIL AT DAWSON CITY, POST OFFICE

E.A.Hegg PHOTO

The stampede slows to a halt

The men on the left are waiting, again, for their mail.
But is that all they are waiting for? The old-timers,
who had seen earlier mining camps rise and then fall,
began to get an uneasy feeling. It was as if the whole
cycle of their experience was being repeated, and this
feeling was communicated to the others, once known as
"cheechakos" – tenderfeet – but who now called themselves
sourdoughs. A sense of anticlimax began to spread.
Had the great adventure finally come to an end?

On the Outside, $5,000 worth of Klondike groceries, hardware, and clothing were dumped on the market at cost. In Dawson, too, the prices were tumbling. Once again men tried to sell their outfits, but here the law of supply and demand, which had once pushed prices up, now brought them down. Who needed to buy a shovel when these lay abandoned by the score along the ravaged valleys of the Klondike?

Waiting and hoping

As the stampede wound down, thousands moved in from the creeks seeking work, but there was less and less work. Now a stale taste began to grow in the mouths of those same men who, a year before, had tumbled from the boats with so much enthusiasm. Some had spent the winter in far-off valleys, working worthless claims, sinking shafts in barren ground. Some had toiled for pay in the filth of the gold creeks, where the glut of men had driven wages down. Some had found jobs in Dawson; some had done nothing. Now, for most, there was nothing left to do but sit on the sidewalk and wait.

OFF FOR CAPE NOME. GOETZMAN
DAWSON.
A.C.CO.
STEAMER.

SEPT.11.

Once again the cry is GOLD!

Suddenly, history repeated itself. A great whisper surged up the Yukon Valley, hinting at a new adventure. In August the rumour was confirmed. A new gold strike had been made on the sands at a place called Nome in Alaska, not far from the Yukon's mouth. Almost instantly, Dawson was emptied as thousands fought for tickets on the riverboats heading for the new find. One gold rush had ended. A new one was about to begin.

9　All That Glitters...

The Klondike fever lasted just two years, from midsummer 1897, when the first news reached the outside world, until midsummer 1899, when the word from Nome emptied Dawson. But in that brief period, thousands of men lived a lifetime. In many ways the great quest was an approximation of life itself, for in its various stages it mirrored the naïveté of childhood, the enthusiasm of youth, the disillusionment of middle age, and the wisdom of maturity. Those who survived the experience and learned from it were made wise; they had taken their own measure and now understood their failings as well as their strengths. At last they realized that the Klondike experience was as much a quest for self as it was for gold.

In the hard university of the trail and the finishing school of the goldfields, they had been made brutally aware of the truth of the familiar copy-book maxims: things are seldom what they seem; a fool and his money are soon parted; more haste, less speed; a friend in need is a friend indeed; all is not gold that glitters.

Most of the high-living Klondike Kings ended their lives in destitution. It was the later arrivals who were the real beneficiaries of the gold rush. The gaudiness of the Klondike adventure was reflected in dozens of success stories: Alexander Pantages opened the continent's best-known theatre chain. Sid Grauman operated Hollywood's most famous movie palace. Wilson Mizner launched the Brown Derby restaurant; his brother Addison was the architect of the Florida land boom. Jack Kearns managed Jack Dempsey. Tex Rickard ran Madison Square Garden. Jack London and Rex Beach wrote best sellers. Joe Boyle became the "Uncrowned King of Rumania." The Klondike also produced a speaker for Canada's House of Commons, a chairman for the u.s. Senate Foreign Relations Committee, a mayor for San Francisco, a premier for British Columbia.

But it was from the shambling ranks of the Front Street parade–the men who had descended into hell and risen again–that the real success stories sprang. A cross-section eventually committed their memories to paper or told them to others, and it is from these that the essence of the Klondike experience can be distilled. The hardship is there, certainly, and also the heartache; but it is muted. The overriding theme is one of exhilaration, of an opportunity not to be missed, of character tempered in the crucible of adversity.

These men had learned that they were capable of feats none could have imagined possible in the years before the stampede. Who today would care to repeat the travail of the gold seekers of Ninety-eight? Who would climb the Chilkoot not once but forty times, with fifty pounds on his back and a blizzard howling in his face? Who would build his own boat of whipsawn spruce and navigate canyon, rapids, and river for five hundred miles? Who would hammer together a hovel of green logs and live on bacon and beans for eight months with the temperature dropping below minus sixty degrees Fahrenheit?

Yet in the space of two crazy seasons, close to thirty thousand men did just that. It would be strange indeed if the experience had not transformed them. Some, as we have seen, were changed for the worse, but the great majority emerged from the North with a new sense of confidence, a new sense of purpose, and above all the sure knowledge that nothing worthwhile in this world is easily gained.

In the quest for Klondike gold, the soft young men photographed in their neat mackinaws and jaunty furs finally lost their innocence.

1897

1899

239